T0265669

PATRIOT PRESIDENTS

LES PRÉSIDENTS DES ETATS-UNIS.
Dédié à leur ami le Général Lafayette.

A French lithograph displays the busts of the first six American presidents above an eagle with a stars and stripes shield and a banner that reads "E Pluribus Unum." Clockwise, from bottom center, are George Washington, John Adams, James Monroe, James Madison, Thomas Jefferson, and John Quincy Adams. *Library of Congress, LC-DIG-pga-07462*

PATRIOT PRESIDENTS

FROM GEORGE WASHINGTON TO JOHN QUINCY ADAMS

WILLIAM E. LEUCHTENBURG

OXFORD
UNIVERSITY PRESS

OXFORD
UNIVERSITY PRESS

Oxford University Press is a department of the University of Oxford. It furthers
the University's objective of excellence in research, scholarship, and education
by publishing worldwide. Oxford is a registered trade mark of Oxford University
Press in the UK and certain other countries.

Published in the United States of America by Oxford University Press
198 Madison Avenue, New York, NY 10016, United States of America.

Library of Congress Cataloging-in-Publication Data
Names: Leuchtenburg, William E. (William Edward), 1922– author.
Title: Patriot presidents : from George Washington to John Quincy Adams /
William E. Leuchtenburg.
Description: New York, NY : Oxford University Press, [2024] |
Includes bibliographical references and index.
Identifiers: LCCN 2024002667 (print) | LCCN 2024002668 (ebook) |
ISBN 9780197598856 (hardback) | ISBN 9780197598870 (epub)
Subjects: LCSH: Presidents—United States—History. |
Presidents—United States—Biography. |
United States—Politics and government—1783–1865. |
United States—History—1783–1865.
Classification: LCC JK511 .L478 2024 (print) | LCC JK511 (ebook) |
DDC 352.23—dc23/eng/20240314
LC record available at https://lccn.loc.gov/2024002667
LC ebook record available at https://lccn.loc.gov/2024002668

DOI: 10.1093/oso/9780197598856.001.0001

Printed by Sheridan Books, Inc., United States of America

For Jean Anne,
My magnificent partner
In this book as in life—
With gratitude for her devotion
and
Admiration for her
Splendid editorial skills

Contents

Preface

The reception of my most recent book, *The American President: From Teddy Roosevelt to Bill Clinton* (Oxford University Press, 2015), has encouraged me to write a multivolume history of the entire US presidency. Since in September 2023 I turned 101 years of age, I recognize that this project may be too ambitious. But I am resolved to carry it through. So I begin, as might be anticipated, with exploring the creation of the institution of the presidency at the 1787 constitutional convention in Philadelphia and the ensuing efforts of the first six incumbents to carry into action the clauses in the founding document. As the historian John C. Miller has observed, "William Penn's aphorism that governments, like clocks, go from the motion given them by men was much in the minds of American Leaders in 1789."

I call these leaders "Patriot" because they were deeply involved in the Patriot cause of the American Revolution and sought to preserve the "Spirit of '76" in their presidencies. George Washington, the esteemed historian Joseph Ellis has written, was "the core of gravity that prevented the American Revolution from flying off into random orbits." His successor, John Adams, had served on the committee that was charged with composing the Declaration of Independence, which the third in line, Thomas Jefferson, had crafted elegantly. Jefferson's ally, James Madison, had made substantial contributions to the interpretation of the Constitution in *The Federalist*, and James Monroe had been grievously wounded as a Patriot soldier. The last of the sextet, John Quincy Adams, was still a boy at the time of the American Revolution, but his mother, Abigail Adams, had made a point of taking him to the battlefield at Bunker Hill, where he saw up close members of the Patriot forces lose their lives to redcoat bullets or bayonets.

A number of historians have recognized the continuum of the war years and the early republic. "The men of 1776," wrote Monroe's biographer Harry Ammon, "did not interpret the American Revolution purely in terms of a severance of the bond with Great Britain, but as a movement to create new institutions radically different from those of the past. They were keenly aware that the epoch about to begin was not only different from all that was past but that it was up to them to make it so."

The Founders seem remote today, despite President Biden's jest about his "friend, Jimmy Madison," but their presidencies provide an instructive measuring rod for twenty-first-century incumbents such as Donald Trump. The exemplary political scientist Thomas E. Cronin has pointed out that "the American presidency is a unique, necessary, yet always possibly dangerous institution. The framers of the Constitution knew this, and we appreciate it as well today. . . . Plainly, to understand the contemporary United States presidency, it is first necessary to understand its creation, the early intentions for it, and how its precedents took shape." No scholar has done so much to demonstrate the enduring significance of eighteenth-century thought as Gordon Wood, who has stated, "Because the sources are so rich and the stakes are so high, interpreting and reinterpreting the constitutional history of the era of the founding will continue just as long as the republic endures." Wood asserts, "In order to establish our nationhood we have to reaffirm and reinforce periodically the values of the men who declared independence from Great Britain and framed the Constitution." Jefferson's biographer, Joseph Ellis, drawing upon an insight of the historian Douglas Adair, has suggested that the Founders "were, in effect, always on their best behavior because they knew we would be watching, an idea we should find endearing because it makes us complicitous in their greatness."

Writing this book has honed my appreciation of fellow historians who have concentrated their scholarship on colonial America and the early republic. Some of them, in turn, may question what I'm doing invading their field, since virtually all of my publications have been about the presidency in the modern, even contemporary, era, especially the long tenure of Franklin Delano Roosevelt. I did, though, steep myself in developments in the early period when I put together an updated version of Samuel Eliot Morison and Henry Steele Commager's classic *The Growth of the American Republic* (Oxford University Press, 1980) and a companion volume, *A Concise History of the American Republic* (Oxford University Press, 1983). I readily acknowledge, however, as I embark on this account of the office which captivates American citizens, that *Patriot Presidents* rests primarily on the recent scholarship of creative and industrious historians.

I

The Constitutional Convention of 1787

Framing the Presidency

At no time in our history has there been so illustrious a gathering as the corps of delegates who came together in the State House (Independence Hall) on Chestnut Street in Philadelphia late in the spring of 1787 to frame a constitution for the United States of America. After Thomas Jefferson, the country's envoy in Paris, ran his eyes over the roster, he wrote his counterpart in London, John Adams, "It really is an assembly of demigods." The convention, agreed Benjamin Franklin, was "*une assemblée des notables*," and J. Hector St. John de Crèvecoeur, born in Normandy to a count and countess, informed the Duc de La Rochefoucauld that the conclave was "composed of the most enlightened men of the continent." Nearly half a century later, Alexis de Tocqueville concluded that mustered in the land's largest city in 1787 were "the choicest talents and the noblest hearts which had ever appeared in the New World." Yet, distinguished though they were, they had only the foggiest notion of how an executive branch should be constructed. Not one of them anticipated the institution of the presidency as it emerged at the end of the summer.

One frightful goblin haunted their deliberations. The study of history—ancient to modern—instructed them that republics were always short-lived, and they feared that America might quickly adopt kingship. "I am told that even respectable characters speak of a monarchical form of Government without horror," the nation's foremost patriot, George Washington, reported with a shudder. "From thinking proceeds speaking, then to acting is often a single step. But how irrevocable and tremendous! what a triumph for our enemies to verify their predictions! what a triumph for the advocates of despotism to find that we are incapable of governing ourselves, and that systems founded on the basis of equal liberty are merely ideal and fallacious!"

Jefferson shared Washington's dismay at that prospect. From Paris, commenting on his experience of three years abroad, he wrote the general: "There is scarcely an evil known in these countries which may not be traced to their king as its source, not a good which is not derived from the small fibres of republicanism existing among them. I can further say with safety, there is not a crowned head in Europe whose talents or merits would entitle him to be elected a vestryman by the people of any parish in America." Little wonder that during the convention proceedings the delegates heard respectfully an orator's exhortation: "May every proposition to add kingly power to our Federal system be regarded as treason to the liberties of our country."

Decades of struggle against royal governors had taught Americans that the executive was their enemy, that legislative assemblies spoke for the people. Hence, in the aftermath of the rebellion against George III, most states had adopted constitutions reflecting the travail of the thirteen colonies. Governors under most of the new state charters were the weakest of sovereigns. They were elected by legislatures, for only a single year; exercised what limited powers they had under the oversight of a council of state chosen by the legislature; and were denied such traditional prerogatives as the veto. New Hampshire would not even tolerate the loathsome word "governor." As James Madison reminded the delegates, "Experience had proved a tendency in our governments to throw all power into the legislative vortex," so that state executives were "little more than cyphers."

The Articles of Confederation drafted during the revolution made no mention at all of an executive. The nonentity designated as president of the Continental Congress had so little authority that when he was absent a clerk took over. He could not make appointments, negotiate treaties, command the armed forces, veto legislation, or pardon, and he did not even have the guarantee of a fixed salary. By 1781, however, a rudimentary executive wing had emerged, with posts filled by men of exceptional ability: Robert Morris as Superintendent of Finance, Robert R. Livingston and then John Jay as Secretary of Foreign Affairs, and Henry Knox as Secretary of War. None of these men, though, was supervised by the figurehead who was called president.

⊷⊶

Yet a good number of the Framers arrived in Philadelphia disenchanted with legislative supremacy and committed to the creation of a potent national government headed by a vigorous executive. They were dismayed by the capture of state governments during the Revolution by crude plebeians who adopted measures that jeopardized property rights. "Smite them," demanded Henry Knox. They wanted a regime strong enough to cope with outbreaks such as Shays's Rebellion—an uprising of debtors in western Massachusetts led by a former captain in the Continental Army—that had prevented courts from convening in Northampton and Worcester and had attempted to seize a federal arsenal. George Washington, who saw this insurrection as proof of the "want of energy" in state governments, railed, "We are fast verging to anarchy and confusion!"

   Despite the fulminations of the Framers against George III, the idea of a strong executive struck a responsive chord. The theorists they read—Blackstone, Locke, Montesquieu—all accepted executive authority. John Locke had written, "The good of the society requires that several things should be left to the discretion of him that has the executive power . . . to be ordered by him as the public good and advantage shall require; nay, it is fit that the laws themselves should in some cases give way to the executive power." Monarchy was the form of government with which Americans were most familiar and hence an inescapable template. Every one of the delegates had been born under the British Crown. South Carolina's Pierce Butler had first come to America as an officer of the redcoats. Wherever they looked in the world, they saw a dominant leader—Catherine the Great ruled Russia, and in Prussia Friedrich der Grosse (Frederick the Great) had died only a year before. New York's constitution authorized a popularly elected governor who was given military command, and Massachusetts, heeding the insistence of the essayist Theophilus Parsons, established a "supreme executive magistrate" personified by John Hancock and James Bowdoin.

Some Americans even dared to think the unthinkable. "Shall we have a king?" John Jay had asked Washington in 1786. A year later, Mercy Otis Warren, who was writing a history of the Revolution, expressed alarm that "the young ardent spirits," especially "the students of Law and the youth of fortune and pleasure," were "ready to bow to the sceptre of a King." Well along in the proceedings at Philadelphia, a North Carolina delegate ventured that it was "pretty certain that we should at some time or other have a King." Yet no one at the convention ever determinedly broached the question of monarchy, not even New York's Alexander Hamilton, who advocated life tenure for the executive and adoption by America of the British style of governance that he thought was the best in the world.

※⋅※

The scaffolding of a presidential office first presented to the delegates for their consideration fell far short of majestic. When toward the end of May Edmund Randolph, the patrician governor of the commonwealth, introduced the Virginia Plan, Resolution Seven provided that "a National Executive be instituted," with no determination of whether the position would be single or plural. It was to be chosen not by popular election but by the National Legislature. The Virginia proposal did not state how many years an executive would serve, but stipulated a single term. He would be granted little more than "a general authority to execute the National laws" and "the Executive rights vested in Congress by the Confederation." Foreign policy and the appointment of officials such as a national treasurer would be entrusted to the legislature.

5. Resolved 'that each branch ought to possess the right of originating acts

6. Resolved. that the national legislature ought to be empowered to enjoy the legislative rights vested in Congress by the confederation — and moreover

to legislate in all cases to which the separate States are incompetent: or in which the harmony of the United States may be interrupted by the exercise of individual legislation.

to negative all laws passed by the several States contravening in the opinion of the national legislature, the articles of union, or any treaties subsisting under the authority of the union.

7. Resolved. that the right of suffrage in the first branch of the national legislature ought not to be according to the rule established in the articles of confederation: but according to some equitable ratio of representation — namely,

in proportion to the whole number of white and other free citizens and inhabitants of every age, sex, and condition including those bound to servitude for a term of years, and three fifths of all other persons not comprehended in the foregoing description, except Indians, not paying taxes in each State.

8. Resolved. that the right of suffrage in the second branch of the national legislature ought to be according to the rule established for the first,

9. Resolved. that a national Executive be instituted to consist of a single Person.

to be chosen by the National Legislature.

for the term of seven years.

with power to carry into execution the national laws

to appoint to Offices in cases not otherwise provided for

to be ineligible a second time, and

to be removable on impeachment and conviction of malpractice or neglect of duty.

to receive a fixed stipend, by which he may be compensated for the devotion of his time to public service

to be paid out of the national Treasury

The Virginia Plan, drafted by James Madison and presented by Edmund Randolph to the Constitutional Convention on May 29, 1787, proposed a strong central government composed of three branches: legislative, executive, and judicial. It envisioned a national executive "to be chosen by the National Legislature[,] for the term of seven years [. . .] to be ineligible a second time, and to be removable on impeachment and conviction of malpractice or neglect of duty." *National Archives, NAID 5730363*

Though the plan bore the name of Governor Randolph, it had largely been devised by James Madison, who had arrived in Philadelphia eleven days early, stealing a march on the other delegates. Not much over five feet in height, Madison, it was said, "was no bigger than a half a piece of soap." Yet "what is very remarkable every Person seems to acknowledge his greatness," a South Carolina delegate noted. "He always comes forward the best informed Man of any point in debate." This "Gentleman of great modesty—with a remarkable sweet temper ... has a most agreeable style of conversation." No one had thought more creatively about constitutional precepts, and no one did so much as he to mount a convincing argument that merely tinkering with the Articles would not suffice. "Never," an English observer said of Madison many years later, "have I seen *so much mind in so little matter.*"

As deliberation on Resolution Seven opened on June 1, the convention got its first indication that, though Madison was on his way toward recognition as father of the Constitution, an unprepossessing Pennsylvanian bent on revamping the Virginia Plan was staking a claim to be regarded as the father of the presidency. Scottish-born James Wilson had studied under the humanists at St. Andrews before migrating at the age of twenty-three to America, where he tutored Latin at the Academy and College of Philadelphia (later the University of Pennsylvania) and read law. Wilson, after winning acclaim for a dazzling pamphlet on the rights of the colonists, was elected to the second Continental Congress and, though a reluctant rebel, became a signer of the Declaration of Independence.

The eminent British scholar Lord Bryce later called Wilson one of the convention's "deepest thinkers and most exact reasoners." Though "no great orator," observed a shrewd fellow delegate, "Mr. Wilson ranks among the foremost in legal and political knowledge. He has joined to a fine genius all that can set him off and show him to advantage. . . . All the political institutions of the world he knows in detail, and can trace the causes and effects of every revolution from the earliest stages of the Grecian commonwealth down to the present time." Wilson's mind, agreed the renowned founding father Benjamin Rush, was "one blaze of light."

Wilson, speaking with a marked Scottish burr, rose to move that a national executive of a single person be established, for a single magistrate could be held accountable to the people. "In order to control the legislative authority, you must divide it," he said. "In order to control the Executive, you must unite it." Steel-rimmed spectacles low on the bridge of his nose, Wilson urged broad authority for an executive who would be a tribune of the people and would give "energy, dispatch, and responsibility to the office."

This motion brought the delegates up short, for Randolph was not alone in seeing in a single executive "the foetus of monarchy." It seemed improbable that Wilson would encounter resistance from the powdered-wigged Pierce Butler, who affected an imperial manner. Proud of his lineage (his mother was a Percy, for centuries one of the most illustrious families in the north of England), he flaunted a gold-laced coat. But Butler, warning that America was not immune from the peril of despotism, asked, "Why might not a Catiline or a Cromwell arise in this country as well as in others?" Another delegate uneasy about concentrated power, the tidewater Virginia patrician George Mason, advocated a three-person executive: one for northern, one for middle, and one for southern states. "Do gentlemen mean to pave the way to hereditary monarchy?" he asked indignantly.

Wilson rejoined that, rather than being the marrow of monarchy, a single executive was the best protection against what a plural executive might well bring: the thirty tyrants of Athens. Wilson's reasoning made sense to other delegates, among them Marblehead's Elbridge Gerry who thought an executive troika "extremely inconvenient . . . particularly in military matters. It would be a general with three heads." With such backing, Wilson prevailed.

Wilson had considerably less success in urging popular election of the executive, an unexpected position for a man who was so distrusted by workingmen in Philadelphia that he had barricaded himself in his lodgings to ward off gunshots during an insurrection in which a number of people were killed. Though Wilson was wary of the populace, he was no less persuaded that empowerment of the people at the polls was vital to the health of the republic. In this advocacy, he was strongly opposed by men such as Roger Sherman, the mayor of New Haven. An artless, self-educated man who eschewed a wig, Sherman nonetheless believed that the people "should have as little to do as may be about government." The "Executive magistracy," he maintained, speaking with a grating Yankee twang, was "nothing more than an institution for carrying the will of the Legislature into effect." The assembly rejected Wilson's motion resoundingly and approved instead choice of the executive by the national legislature (not yet called "Congress") for a single term of seven years.

Surprisingly, the convention contemplated vesting in that single executive the power of vetoing legislation. The colonists had been incensed by the exercise of that prerogative by royal governors, and the first charge in the Declaration of Independence against George III was that he had "refused his Assent to Laws, the most wholesome and necessary for the public good." But recent experience with legislative caprice persuaded the delegates that there needed to be some check. Consequently, the executive was given a limited veto that could be overridden by a proportion of members of the legislature eventually established as two-thirds of both houses. The word "veto," though, appears nowhere in the Constitution.

These decisions did not end the matter. In the course of the convention, the delegates were to go through sixty ballots before resolving how to choose a president. No sooner did they come to a conclusion than they voted to undo it. In mid-summer, Gerry acknowledged, "We seem to be entirely at a loss on this head." As the political scientist Robert Dahl has written, "The Convention twisted and turned like a man tormented in his sleep by a bad dream as it tried to decide." Not until the final days would the issue be settled.

The convention conducted all of its work in secrecy because delegates sought to be free to change their minds without inviting charges of waffling and because they did not want anyone to know what mischief they were up to. Authorized only to propose amendments to the Articles, they were instead creating an entirely new charter in what the historian Garry Wills has called this "treasonous project of giving us our Constitution." With windows clamped shut to assure privacy, wool-suited Yankee delegates sweltered in the stifling midsummer heat, while the country brooded about what might be transpiring week after week in "the dark conclave."

In August, suspicion that the delegates were plotting to impose a king on the new republic reached a crescendo. Rumors gained credence that the convention planned to call to a throne in America the Bishop of Osnaburgh, a Hanoverian cleric who was the second son of George III. The delegates regarded this alarum so seriously that, for the only time during the proceedings, they transmitted information to the press, stating, "We are well informed that many letters have been written to the members of the federal convention from different quarters, respecting the reports idly circulating, that it is intended to establish a monarchical government, to send for the Bishop of Osnaburgh, etc., etc.—to which it has been uniformly answered, 'Tho we cannot, affirmatively, tell you what we are doing; we can, negatively, tell you what we are not doing—we never once thought of a King.'"

At the very time that the Osnaburgh canard was being noised about, the delegates were resolving not to exalt executive authority but to constrain it. When a Committee of Detail reported on August 6, it left the executive, who now bore a new title, "President of the United States of America," a creature of Congress. He could never claim a popular mandate, for Congress, not the people, would select him. Furthermore, the Senate was given exclusive charge of foreign affairs (long regarded as the domain of the head of state) and was empowered to appoint ambassadors and judges.

Over the next few weeks, however, a number of delegates—conspicuously Wilson, Madison, and South Carolina's Charles Pinckney III—had qualms about a fettered executive and a Senate cabal. Earlier, in impressive orations, Pennsylvania's Gouverneur

Morris, though no democrat, had maintained that the executive must be fully equipped to become "the guardian of the people, even of the lower classes" against "Legislative tyranny," because the "Great and wealthy . . . in the course of things will necessarily compose the Legislative body." So on the final day of August the convention created a Committee on Postponed Matters to sort out the institution of the presidency.

In the first week of September, when the Framers took up the question of the presidency for a final time, they revised many of their previous decisions, especially in order to adjust the imbalance between the chief executive and Congress. They authorized the president to appoint major officials, including ambassadors and Supreme Court justices, and they turned over to him the right to make treaties, though with the advice and consent of two-thirds of the Senate. By agreeing to Pinckney's proposal that the president "shall, by Virtue of his Office, be Commander in Chief of the Land Forces of U.S. and Admiral of their Navy," they gave him immense power to determine strategy in wartime and in other national emergencies, thus establishing the principle of civilian supremacy over the military.

The convention stopped well short of investing him with monarchical authority, however. Sir William Blackstone would have been shocked to learn that the Framers denied the president what, in his seminal *Commentaries on the Laws of England*, he had seen as a fundamental privilege of rulers: "the sole prerogative of making war and peace." Instead, delegates lodged the war power with Congress. Jefferson rejoiced in this "effectual check to the dog of war by transferring the power of letting him loose, from the executive to the legislative body," and a decade after the Philadelphia meeting Madison explained: "The constitution supposes, what the History of all Govts demonstrates, that the Ex. is the branch of power most interested in war, & most prone to it. It has accordingly with studied care vested the question of war in the Legisl."

This feature, though, proved less decisive than it seemed. Madison won acceptance for substituting "declare" for "make" war, thereby "leaving to the Executive the power to repel sudden attacks," and also eliminating the possibility that "make" might be thought to mean "conduct." Furthermore, in only five instances over the next two centuries were US armed forces employed as a consequence of a Congressional declaration. Instead, presidents seized the initiative or involved the nation in an imbroglio so deeply that Congress had no choice but to go along.

The Committee on Postponed Matters made a critical move in taking choice of the president from Congress and vesting it in an "electoral college." It refined a proposal that James Wilson had aired earlier by requiring that electors meet in their respective states. Thus "college" was a misnomer from the outset; it was never intended to be a deliberative body that debated the merits of candidates. Each state would have as many electors as it had members in the two houses of Congress, an ingenious formula that gave larger states the heftier clout but overrepresented small states by crediting each with its two senators, regardless of the size of its population. "The small states," one scholar later remarked, "had demanded and obtained their pound of flesh." Electors would "vote by ballot for two persons," one of whom had to be from another state.

The person with the second highest number would become vice president. ("Such an office as vice-President was not wanted," stated North Carolina's Hugh Williamson. "He was introduced only for the sake of a valuable mode of election which required two to be chosen at the same time.") The vice president would preside over the Senate, and, in the event of the death or incapacity of the president, would exercise the powers of the office. If none of the candidates obtained a majority of electoral votes, the determination would revert to the House, with each state's delegation entitled to one vote. In practice, Mason reckoned, the House would wind up choosing the president "nineteen times in twenty." The Electoral College, the historian Gordon Wood has concluded, "was an ingenious solution to delicate and controversial political problems, and the fact that it has rarely worked the way it was intended does not change its ingeniousness."

Never did the Framers seriously entertain direct popular election of the president—not simply, as is so often said, because they abhorred democracy. The great expanse of the country, Mason contended not unreasonably, made it "impossible that the people can have the requisite capacity to judge of the respective pretensions of the Candidates." Gloucester fishermen in pursuit of cod on the Grand Banks could not imagine the lives of Philadelphia cordwainers or South Carolina indigo planters, let alone pass judgment on the political figures in those orbits. Furthermore, delegates from small states feared that the winner of a plebiscite would always come from one of the more populous states. Indirect election also militated against the emergence of a demagogue inflaming or truckling to the masses. There was in addition, though, a strong current of contempt for the judgment of the hoi polloi. Mason thought "it were as unnatural to refer the choice of a . . . chief magistrate to the people, as it would be to refer a trial of colours to a blind man."

The convention fixed a president's term at four years, but, altering its previous arrangement, agreed that a president would be perpetually eligible for re-election. A president chosen by Congress, Mason had earlier reasoned, should be restricted to only one term in order to eliminate the "temptation on the part of the Executive to intrigue with the Legislature for a re-appointment." But once the choice was removed from the legislature, that objection ceased to be relevant. Gouverneur Morris saw more than one advantage to re-eligibility of a president. The country would not lose a good man after just one term; an incumbent would have "the great motive to good behavior, the hope of being rewarded with a re-appointment"; and the country would elude a predicament: "Shut the Civil road to Glory & he may be compelled to seek it by the sword."

Once these large matters had been disposed of, the delegates made a quick meal of the remaining details. The president was required to be "a natural born Citizen, or a Citizen of the United States, at the time of the adoption of this Constitution," at least thirty-five years of age, and a resident of the United States for fourteen years. (These provisions eliminated any possibility that a Bishop of Osnaburgh would surface or that Tories who had fled the country could return and reach for the highest office.) No minimum property-owning or religious qualifications were imposed. The president could "require the Opinion, in writing, of the principal Officer in each of the executive Departments" (a clause that is the seedbed of the cabinet); was empowered to grant pardons; could convene Congress "on extraordinary Occasions"; could receive ambassadors; and "shall from time to time give to the Congress Information of the State of the Union." He could be removed by impeachment for, and conviction of treason, bribery, or other high crimes and misdemeanors. The House was authorized to impeach (indict), the Senate to conduct the ensuing trial; a two-thirds vote of the Senate would be necessary to oust a president.

The delegates assigned the task of polishing the draft of the Constitution to a committee of style chaired by the redoubtable Gouverneur Morris. A patrician to his fingertips, Morris was son of the lord of the manor of Morrisania northeast of Manhattan. (His French first name derived from his mother's family, which was Huguenot.) After a spat with the governor of New York, Gouverneur Morris had removed to Philadelphia. Despite a peg leg, "The Tall Boy," stomping about on his wooden limb while brandishing a cane, cut an impressive figure. Commentators reported that he had numerous sexual conquests. (It was rumored falsely that he had lost his leg by leaping from a balcony to elude an irate husband. "I am almost tempted to wish," commented John Jay, that the rake "had lost *something else.*") Morris's nature, said a Revolutionary War officer, "admitted of no alliance with despondency." When a Shaker preacher sermonized that Morris should abandon "the conjugal pleasures," he rejected the counsel as an "unnatural (and therefore impious) doctrine."

No one doubted that he was bright. He had enrolled at King's College (which would become Columbia University) at twelve and was graduated at sixteen. A critic said that at the Continental Congress Morris was "an eternal speaker and for brass unequalled," and at the constitutional convention he spoke more times than anyone else. But he was not garrulous; he just had a lot to say. "Mr. Gouverneur Morris," observed a Southern delegate, "is one of those Geniuses in whom every species of talents combine. . . . He . . . throws around him such a glare that he charms, captivates, and leads away the senses of all who hear him. . . . But with all these powers he is fickle and inconstant—never pursuing one train of thinking—nor ever regular." When George Washington found it necessary to inform Morris that he had been charged "with levity and imprudence of conversation and conduct," Morris acknowledged that "circumspection of conduct . . . has hitherto . . . formed no part of my character."

As the most important member of the Committee on Style and Arrangement, Morris did more than tidy up straggling sentences. Together with Madison, Hamilton, William Samuel Johnson, who would become president of King's College, and the eloquent Massachusetts delegate Rufus King, he imparted, as he acknowledged, his own ideas of proper government. Gouverneur Morris, one scholar later said, had "a strong claim to share paternity of the Presidency." In particular, Morris's committee crafted the portentous opening sentence of Article II.

Article II begins, "The executive Power shall be vested in a President of the United States of America." The sentence seems innocuous, merely descriptive. But it contrasts starkly with a companion sentence in Article I: "All legislative Powers *herein granted* shall be vested in a Congress of the United States." Is the absence of the restriction "herein granted" in Article II merely chance phrasing, or is it evidence of Gouverneur Morris's cunning? No matter—for presidents have seized upon this phrasing to claim powers not enumerated in the Constitution. They have issued proclamations, acted in emergencies without seeking Congressional approval, and entered into executive agreements with foreign nations. In the first century of the republic, executive agreements were nearly as frequent as treaties, and in the next half-century they outnumbered treaties by almost 2–1. Article II further provides that "he shall take Care that the Laws be faithfully executed," another innocent-sounding clause pregnant with potential for amplifying the presidential realm.

Perhaps not guilelessly, the committee fashioning Article II created, as the political scientist E. S. Corwin later noted, "the most loosely drawn chapter of the Constitution." He added: "To those who think that a constitution ought to settle everything beforehand, it should be a nightmare; by the same token, to those who think that constitution makers ought to leave considerable leeway for the future play of political forces, it should be a vision realized." Similarly, the British historian Marcus Cunliffe later remarked, "Napoleon once said that constitutions should be 'short and obscure.' . . . Much in the Constitution was vague, either because the delegates covered up disagreement with . . . words open to multiple interpretation, or because they were not able to anticipate the vast range of difficulties that would arise when the Constitution was tested." Article II is confoundingly silent about which administrators fall under the president's authority, and the executive branch is nowhere mentioned, though it is adumbrated.

The committee also altered the wording of the preface of the Constitution. Initially, it read, "We the people of New Hampshire, Massachusetts, . . ." and so forth southward down the Atlantic coast. In its revised form, the preface announced, "We the people of the United States. . . ." The preface has no heft in law courts because it does not grant or allot power. But the revised wording conveyed the message that the Founders wanted it understood that they were creating not a confederation of states but a new nationalist structure.

To the dismay of opponents of concentrated authority such as George Mason, the Framers had also bestowed plenary powers on the president. When Charles Pinckney III expressed disappointment at "the contemptible weakness and dependence of the executive," Mason gasped. Advocates of an energetic executive, though, applauded the empowerment. "The duration of our president," said John Adams, "is neither perpetual nor for life; it is only for four years; but his power during those four years is much greater than that of an avoyer, a consul, a podesta, a doge, a stadtholder, nay, than a king of Poland; nay,

Howard Chandler Christy's monumental painting, *Signing of the Constitution of the United States*, is displayed in the east grand stairway of the House wing of the US Capitol. George Washington stands on the dais that he occupied throughout the proceedings of the Constitutional Convention. Seated in the center is Benjamin Franklin. Alexander Hamilton leans toward him, and James Madison appears farther to the right. *Architect of the Capitol*

than a king of Sparta." Unlike Congress, which, for months at a time, would be adjourned, the president would hold sway throughout the year. Subsequently, a congressman inquired: "Is anything more plain than that the President, above all the officers of Government, both from the manner of his appointment, and the nature of his duties, is truly and justly denominated the man of the people? Is there any other person who represents so many of them as the President?"

⁘

A week later, Congress sent the Constitution to the states, where it encountered vigorous objections in unexpected quarters. Though the Constitution had originated in the Virginia Plan, Virginians—among them Randolph and a future president, James Monroe—voiced vehement disapproval of a powerful presidency. If Richard Henry Lee, author of the anti-federalist "Letters of the Federal Farmer," who shared these objections, was the Cicero of Virginia, as one historian has said, the illustrious Virginia orator Patrick Henry was the Demosthenes. Henry, a stenographer recorded, "strongly and pathetically expatiated on the probability of the President's enslaving America, and the horrid consequences that must result." Henry did in fact declare, "The Constitution is said to have beautiful features, but when I come to examine these features, Sir, they appear to me to be horridly frightful. Among other deformities, . . . it squints toward monarchy."

Critics in other states joined the Virginians in regretting that the Constitution did not limit a president to one term. Troubled by the thought that the president could be re-elected infinitely, a South Carolina legislator remonstrated, "You don't even put the same check on him that you do on your own state governor; a man . . . bred among you—a man over whom you have a continual and watchful eye— . . . this man you say shall not be elected for more than four years, and yet this mighty—this omnipotent governor general may be elected for years and years." From Paris, Jefferson, vexed about a president's re-eligibility, wrote Washington, "This, I fear, will make an office for life.

I was much an enemy of monarchy before I came to Europe. I am ten thousand times more so since I have seen what they are."

Speculation that the presidency might encompass lifetime tenure nourished the conviction that the Framers had cleared the way for the second coming of a George III. In a series of articles in a Philadelphia journal, a critic called the president "this *tyrant*" armed with powers "exceeding those of the most *despotic monarch* . . . in modern times." One South Carolina legislator foresaw that a president could hold the office "so long that it will be impossible without a revolution to displace him." So probable did it seem to some that under this Constitution the country would before long be crowning a king that still another South Carolinian wanted his family seal authenticated in England, "for as our steps toward monarchy are very obvious, I would wish my Children to have all the Rights to rank, & distinction, which is to be claimed from Ancestry."

Supporters of the Constitution rebutted these assumptions. In *The Federalist*, a seminal collection of essays by three of the Founders, Alexander Hamilton, the primary author, met the objection to re-eligibility of presidents by asking whether it would serve the public weal to have numbers of ex-presidents "wandering among the people like discontented ghosts and sighing for a place they were destined never more to possess." And when Jefferson wrote John Adams that he was worried about the re-eligibility of a president, Adams responded, "You are apprehensive the President, when once chosen, will be cho-sen again and again as long as he lives. So much the better, it appears to me."

In *The Federalist*, Hamilton derided writers who had been carica-turing the president as an absolute monarch. He wrote mockingly:

> He has been shown to us with the diadem sparkling on his brow and the imperial purple flowing in his train. He has been seated on a throne surrounded with minions and mistresses, giving audience to the envoys of foreign potentates, in all the supercilious pomp of majesty. The images of Asiatic despotism and voluptuousness have scarcely been wanting to crowd the exaggerated scene. We have been taught to tremble at the

terrific visages of murdering janizaries and to blush at the unveiled mysteries of the seraglio.

Scoffing at the accusation that the president would be identical to the king of Great Britain, Hamilton underscored the many differences. A president would serve for four years; a king served for life. Kingship was hereditary; the presidency was not. A president was subject to impeachment; the person of a king was inviolable. A king had an absolute veto on legislation; a president only a qualified one. A king could declare war and raise armies and navies on his own authority; these powers were reserved by the Constitution to Congress. A king was "the *sole possessor* of the power of making treaties"; a president had to share that right with the Senate. A king was "the sole author of all appointments"; a president required the approval of the legislative branch. A king could "make denizens of aliens, noblemen of commoners"; a president had "no privileges whatsoever" to bestow. A president had "no particle of spiritual jurisdiction; the other is supreme head and governor of the national church!"

Though there was enough clamor to induce Hamilton to offer his confutation, what is striking is how relatively little of the animus toward the Constitution was directed at provisions for the presidency—in large measure because of the universal assumption that the first incumbent would be George Washington. After taking leave of his officers in a moving ceremony at Fraunces Tavern in lower Manhattan, the wartime commander had retired to his plantation "on the banks of the Patowmac . . . under my own Vine and my own Fig-tree, free from the bustle of the camp and the intrigues of a court," and there he had intended to "glide gently down the stream of life" for the rest of his days. But something needed to be done, he acknowledged, "to avert the humiliating and contemptible figure we are about to make on the annals of mankind."

So disturbed was Washington about the dearth of leadership that he had consented to go to Philadelphia, where he became the inevitable choice to preside over the constitutional convention. If hesitant delegates brooded about granting authority that might be abused, all they needed to do was look at the reticent figure who took his seat in the high-backed chair on the dais each morning and quietly presided, almost never intruding into the debates. The powers of the president are "full great," Pierce Butler observed later, "and greater than I was disposed to make them. Nor, *entre nous*, do I believe they would have been so great had not many of the members cast their eyes towards General Washington as president; and shaped their Ideas of the Powers to be given a President, by their opinions of his Virtue." The prospect that Washington would be the country's first chief executive may well account for why, though sometimes by very narrow margins, the states ratified the Constitution, a consummation formally announced on July 2, 1788. "Washington's name carried the day," Monroe said resignedly.

George Washington, venerated as the hero of the War of Independence—of the doughty Christmas night crossing of the icy Delaware, of the harsh winter ordeal at Valley Forge, of the glorious triumph at Yorktown—was swiftly rising to the status of a deity. In 1783, the president of Yale, Ezra Stiles, had intoned: "O Washington! How I do love thy name! How have I often adored and blessed thy God, for creating and forming thee the great ornament of human kind!" On meeting Washington, Abigail Adams, no sentimentalist, found that she was instantly reminded of John Dryden's lines:

> Mark his majestic fabric; he's a temple
> > Sacred by birth, and built by hands divine;
> His soul's the deity that lodges there;
> > Nor is the pile unworthy of the God.

The universal cry for Washington to become president encountered just one obstacle: he had no intention of accepting the honor. He had sacrificed years to public service, and he wanted to spend whatever time might be left him in private pursuits. "I have but one wish myself, which is to live & die on my own plantation," he told a former aide-de-camp. He genuinely doubted that he was the person for the post. "I think there are a great many men in the U.S. much fitter for the office than I am," he said. "I cannot pretend to be so well acquainted with civil matters, as I was with military affairs." He was also jealous of his reputation. To take on the presidency opened the risk of denunciation, for he was wise enough to recognize that heading an untried government would inevitably engender "ten thousand embarrassments, perplexities and troubles" upon which defamers would swarm. Furthermore, at Fraunces Tavern he had renounced all ambition for preferment. Would not departing from that pledge now seem perfidious? Surely he had served enough years to have his desire for repose respected.

The general's reluctance only magnified his appeal. Nothing about him suggested a man on horseback, lusting for power. In March 1783, when commander of the Revolutionary Army, he had put down the Newburgh Conspiracy of mutinous officers who had sought to disperse Congress and place Washington on a throne. Anyone "who wickedly attempts to open the floodgates of civil discord and deluge our rising empire in blood" should be denounced, he declared. "Farmer Washington," a toastmaster offered at a Fourth of July celebration, "may he like a second Cincinnatus be called from the plow to rule a great people." The comparison to the ancient Roman had become commonplace, for Washington, too, had left his crops in the field to lead an army, then eschewed the opportunity for power and returned to the plow.

From every quarter, Washington heard that he had no choice save to accept the summons. "Your cool steady Temper is *indispensably necessary* to give a firm and manly Tone to the new Government," Gouverneur Morris told him. "No Constitution is the same on Paper and in Life. The Exercise of Authority depends on personal Character." Hamilton shrewdly played on his fear that his reputation would be sullied by telling him that it would be "inglorious in such a situation not to hazard the glory, however great, which he might have previously acquired." Entreaties came even from the French aristocrat Lafayette, who had volunteered for the Patriot army and had commanded Revolutionary troops at Yorktown. "I beseech you, my dear General, not to deny your acceptance of the office of President for the first years," the marquis wrote him. "You only can settle that political machine."

⊹⊱

While Washington temporized, the Electoral College swung into action. Voting in their separate states, every one of the sixty-nine electors marked his ballot for the general. (They scattered their second ballots among several choices, but, since John Adams had the highest total, though less than half as many as Washington, he became vice president, a dubious distinction. The vice president, declared Benjamin Franklin, might appropriately be addressed as "His Superfluous Excellency.") As word of the first election returns drifted in, Washington confided, "I feel very much like a man who is condemned to death does when the time of his execution draws nigh."

A more ambitious man would have hastened to the capital, but Washington, scrupulous to the end, stayed home until the election had been certified and he had been officially notified. Congress did not secure a quorum until April 6, 1789, when, with members of both houses attending, the president pro tem of the Senate opened and counted the ballots. It took more than a week thereafter for a courier to reach Mount Vernon with news of the election. Two days later, Washington entered in his diary: "About ten o'clock I bade adieu to Mount Vernon, to private life, and to domestic felicity, and, with a mind oppressed with more anxious and painful sensations than I have words to express, set out for New York." He resolved to do so at a slow pace so that he would not seem "improperly eager for the office."

Washington's eight-day journey to the inauguration ceremony in New York, the country's first capital, gave every appearance of a triumphal tour befitting a Roman emperor. The citizens of Alexandria, Virginia, sent him on his way north with a farewell banquet at Wise's Tavern where thirteen toasts (one for each state) were capped by an address from the mayor who counseled the general, "Go and make

In this lithograph by Nathaniel Currier, George Washington is feted by ladies on the bridge at Trenton, New Jersey, where he won a significant victory in the American Revolution after crossing the icy Delaware River. He is on his way to New York City to be inaugurated as the first president of the United States. *Library of Congress, LC-DIG-ppmsca-07649*

a grateful people happy!" His hosts shepherded him in his carriage on a ferry across the Potomac, where they entrusted him to a delegation of affectionate Marylanders. The boom of artillery welcomed him to Baltimore, and when he departed—again to the cannons' roar—an honor guard escorted him for seven miles toward Delaware. The burgesses of Wilmington, in turn, bade him Godspeed at the Pennsylvania border, and, on reaching Philadelphia, the city fathers provided him with a magnificently caparisoned white steed which he cantered down Market Street to the hosannas of twenty thousand citizens. He entered Trenton under a towering arch of greenery, and, after a white-robed choir serenaded him, young women with baskets of flowers strewed blossoms in his path.

None of these expressions of adulation, though, prepared Washington for the reception that greeted him on his approach to New York and within that first capital. As he sailed across the bay from New Jersey in a festooned barge, propelled by thirteen sailors in white smocks, accompanied by a flotilla of brightly decorated small craft, a sloop pulled alongside so that choristers could sing odes of praise. "At this moment," a member of the welcoming committee wrote his wife, "a number of porpoises came playing amongst us, as if they had risen up to know what was the cause of all this happiness. We now discovered the shores to be crowded with thousands of people—men, women, and children—nay, I may venture to say, tens of thousands . . . thick as ears of corn before the harvest."

When the barge docked at the foot of Manhattan Island, church bells pealed and a salvo of thirteen-gun salutes drew three ringing cheers from the immense throng there to laud him. The huzzahs were, without doubt, intended to pay homage to the commander who was revered as America's liberator, but they also signified something more—a keen sensibility that in not many days the figure they were acclaiming would be sworn in as the first president of their newborn republic, a man who would govern under a written constitution.

2

George Washington

Launching the Presidency

"Do you solemnly swear," asked New York's highest judicial officer, Chancellor Robert Livingston, "that you will faithfully execute the office of President of the United States and will, to the best of your ability, preserve, protect, and defend the Constitution of the United States?" As the huge crowd milling below the canopied portico of Federal Hall at the corner of Wall and Nassau Streets in Manhattan looked up expectantly, George Washington, one hand raised toward the sky, the other on a Bible resting on a crimson cushion, repeated the oath—and added, according to a later account, "so help me God," kissing the Bible. It would have been uncharacteristic of the general to say "God" because he was more likely to allude to "the Great Author of every public and private good," "the benign parent of the human race," or some similar circumlocution, but his behavior initiated a tradition of linking the fate of the republic to the benevolence of the Lord, who had upmost on his mind the welfare of the United States of America.

"Long live George Washington, President of the United States," Livingston cried when the ceremony on this thirtieth day of April in 1789 ended, and the noisily cheering throng echoed his words, calling out, "God bless our Washington! Long live our beloved president!" The raising of a flag over the building signaled gunners at the Battery to let loose a thirteen-gun fusillade, which was matched by salvos

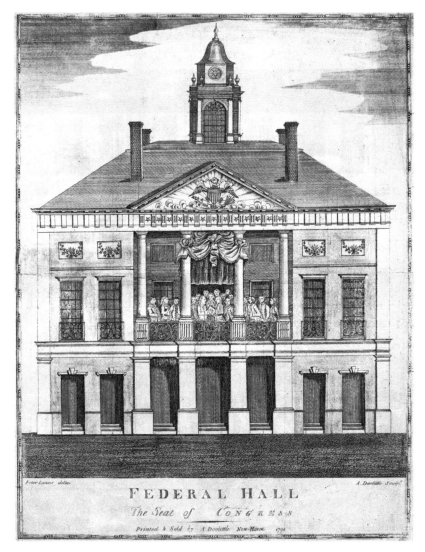

FEDERAL HALL
The Seat of CONGRESS
Printed & Sold by A. Doolittle New-Haven 1790

George Washington takes the oath of office on April 30, 1789, in this engraving by Amos Doolittle. The ceremony took place in Federal Hall in New York City, the nation's first capital. "Federalism" refers to the sharing of powers between national and state governments, but in this instance "federal" indicates the authority of the national government only. In the years after Washington's inauguration, federal hegemony expanded. *The New York Public Library Digital Collections,* digitalcollections.nypl.org/items/ 510d47d9-7b06-a3d9-e040-e00a18064a99 from a Spanish warship in the harbor. Never, the French envoy Count de Moustier reported, had a "sovereign reigned more completely in the hearts of his subjects than did Washington in those of his fellow citizens.... He has the soul, look, and figure of a hero united in him."

Amid the din, Washington, after bowing to the citizenry, strode from the portico into the lavish Senate chamber, where, seeming "agitated and embarrassed more than ever he was by the leveled cannon or pointed musket," he presented a brief inaugural address, one of his many precedent-creating innovations, for the Constitution makes no mention of such an obligation. (Subsequent inaugurations would also draw upon other actions he took that day: his procession to the oath taking; the plein air ceremony; the gala in the evening.) He alluded to himself as "one . . . inheriting inferior endowments from nature and unpracticed in the duties of civil administration." Sensitive to how fragile was this experiment in self-rule, he maintained that "the sacred fire of liberty, and the destiny of the republican model of government, are justly considered as deeply, perhaps as finally staked, on the experiment entrusted to . . . the American people."

Congress in turn delivered formal responses. (Congressman James Madison helped draft both the president's address and the response.) One US senator recorded in his journal:

> The Senate met. The Vice President rose in the most solemn manner. . . . "Gentlemen, I wish for the direction of the Senate. The President will, I suppose, address the Congress. How shall I behave? How shall we receive it? Shall I be standing or sitting?"
>
> . . . Mr. Lee began with the House of Commons (as is usual with him), then the House of Lords, then the King, and then back again. The result of his information was that the Lords sat and the Commons stood on the delivery of the King's speech.

These jejune imitations of the king's speech from the throne and of the rejoinder modeled on those from the houses of Parliament gave only one indication of how hard it was for the new government to establish republican rituals. Washington's garb also revealed a young nation in transition. He wore, appropriately, a simple double-breasted

brown suit of broadcloth spun in Hartford, but he had seen to it
that his hair was powdered, his shoe buckles silver, his stockings fine
silk, his suit adorned with gilt buttons, and, later, that he was orna-
mented with dress sword and steel scabbard—trappings suggestive of
a European court. In New York, and the country's successor capital,
Philadelphia, white stallions with saddles draped in gold bunting and
embellished with his coat of arms—a griffin, symbol of heraldry—
would draw his ornate carriage, accompanied by four liveried out-
riders. On a subsequent tour of nearly two thousand miles through
the South, he entered each town mounted on his white steed, Prescott,
whose hooves had been painted, and he was accompanied by a grey-
hound, saucily called Cornwallis. His household attendants included
seven slaves. Commentators called his inauguration a coronation,
and he was toasted as "His Highness." His wife Martha made a royal
journey from Mount Vernon to New York, where she was hailed as
"Lady Washington."

The Senate, too, reflected this inclination toward royalty. At a time
when it should have been concentrating on getting the new government underway, it bogged down for three weeks in a prolix argument over the proper form of address for the chief executive. Vice
President John Adams, speaking from the dais, harangued legislators to accept a ponderous formulation: "His Highness the President
of the United States and Protector of their Liberties." If the country's chief magistrate were merely called "President of the United
States," as in Article II, "the common people of foreign countries, . . .
the sailors and soldiers . . . will despise him to all eternity," Adams
maintained. Senator Oliver Ellsworth of Connecticut agreed. There
were, after all, presidents "of Fire Companies & of a Cricket Club."
The Senate approved Adams's cumbersome formulation, but the
House of Representatives, guided by Madison, insisted on the simple
"President of the United States." George Washington, Madison was
sure, wanted no one "to bedizen him with a . . . spurious title" and so
it has been ever since. President Washington, who in truth was slow

to object, concluded, "Happily the matter is now done with, I hope never to be reviewed."

Though Adams lost this particular contest, he made the most of his role as president of the US Senate. He presided over the upper chamber in powdered wig and flaunted a small sword. He also insisted on participating vigorously in Senate debates, activities that his successors eschewed. Adams reached his post in an imposing carriage drawn by six horses with a driver in livery, and he continued to maintain that the government of the republic merited "dignity and Splendor." (Over the course of time, however, he resigned himself to being, in the historian Joseph Ellis's words, "muzzled and largely ignored in the vice presidency." On one occasion, Adams stated, "Gentlemen, I feel a great difficulty how to act. I am vice president. In this I am nothing, but I may be everything.")

The persona of the first president had, much more conspicuously, elements of the monarchical. A man capable of fiery passion, Washington projected toward the world a remoteness so stony that he might already have been settling into his image in Houdon's marble sculpture. When the wife of the British ambassador said that his face revealed his emotions, he rejoined, "You are wrong. My countenance never yet betrayed my feelings." He understood that he was to govern, but he also recognized that the American president is head of state as well as chief executive. He sought to attain a level between "lowering the dignity and respect that was due to the first Magistrate" and "an ostentatious shew of mimicry of sovereignty." Washington, reported a visiting Englishman, "has something uncommonly majestic and commanding in his walk, his address, his figure, and his countenance." His great stature and formidable presence led Benjamin Rush to say that "there is not a king in Europe that would not look like a *valet de chambre* by his side."

Washington comprehended, though, that he officiated in a republic and tried to respond appropriately, if with scant success. Afternoons, he would take it on himself to depart from his office and walk the streets of the capital, opening himself to conversing with the citizenry.

George Washington in a 1796 portrait by Gilbert Stuart. His black velvet suit and shirt with white ruffles accorded him a grandeur his followers thought appropriate for a leader who was displacing a monarch, but distanced him from the American people. Through the ages, Washington has been much admired but has seemed remote and inaccessible. *National Portrait Gallery, Smithsonian Institution, acquired as a gift to the nation through the generosity of the Donald W. Reynolds Foundation, NPG.2001.13*

On one occasion, he came upon six-year-old Washington Irving. The lad's Scottish caretaker, speaking to the president, said, "Here's a bairn was named after you." (A generation later, Irving would write a biography of George Washington.) It is hard to bring to mind another ruler in the world who would mingle with the populace so casually, save, of course, for Good King Wenceslas.

In fact, Washington adopted a more formal mode of communication. To make himself accessible, he scheduled levees (a term of the Crown) open to any respectably dressed man, and he turned up faithfully at his wife's weekly drawing room (women as well as men, no invitation needed; ice cream and lemonade served as well as tea or coffee). But the levees were such stiffish affairs that critics grumbled that the president was mimicking a European court with "all the faulty finery, brilliant scenes and expensive trappings of Royal Government." The president, hair powdered, received guests in formal black velvet dress adorned with sword in white leather scabbard. The sword occupied one hand and, with a bogus feather contraption intended to resemble a hat in the other, he was able to fend off any caller who thought to become too familiar by attempting to shake his hand. It was said that there was more pomp at these levees than at St. James's, the British royal court. The poet John Turnbull, who had expressed admiration for Washington, deplored "the odour of incense" at the inauguration ceremony and the subsequent "Popish grades of worship" of the president.

The perception of George Washington even took on some of the aspects of the former monarch. In Washington Irving's beloved tale, the Dutch character Rip Van Winkle awakens from the American Revolution, which he has slept through. When he returns to his hometown, he finds the sign over the inn familiar for it features "the ruby face of King George, under which he had smoked so many a peaceful pipe, but," Irving writes, "this was singularly metamorphosed. The red coat was changed for one of blue and buff, a sword was held in the hand instead of a scepter, the head was decorated with a cocked hat, and underneath was painted in large characters, GENERAL WASHINGTON."

Though Washington may never have been deeply influenced by the British political theorist Henry St. John, First Viscount Bolingbroke, he emanated the aura of Bolingbroke's patriot king: a man above faction who would, in Bolingbroke's words, "put himself at the head of his people in order to govern, or more properly to subdue, all parties." Gordon Wood has said of Washington, "Not only did he have to justify and flesh out the new office of the presidency, but he also had to put together the new nation and prove to a skeptical world that America's grand experiment in self-government was possible. That he did all this in the midst of a revolutionary world at war and did it without sacrificing the republican character of the country is an astonishing achievement, one that the achievements of no other president, however great, can begin to match."

➵➴

The first American president began his tenure acutely aware that every step he took might affect not only his constituents but also millions yet unborn who would inherit the institutions he had the awesome responsibility of helping to create. "Few who are not philosophical Spectators," he observed, "can realize the difficult and delicate part which a man in my situation has to act. . . . In our progress toward political happiness my station is new; and . . . I walk on *untrodden ground*. . . . There is scarcely any part of my conduct which may not hereafter be drawn into precedent." He remarked to John Adams, "Many things which appear of little importance in themselves . . . may have great and durable consequences from their having been established at the commencement of a new general government."

Washington also saw these first steps as having worldwide significance. He instructed the Pennsylvania legislature: "It should be the highest ambition of every American to extend his views beyond himself, and to bear in mind that his conduct will not only affect himself, his country, and his immediate posterity, but that its influence may be co-extensive with the world, and stamp political happiness or misery on ages yet unborn." He concluded, "We may reasonably hope, under the smiles of Heaven, to convince the world that the happiness of nations can be accomplished by pacific revolutions in their political systems, without the destructive intervention of the sword."

Under Washington, the framework of a national government emerged, though in fits and starts. In creating the first of the executive departments in 1789, Congress carried on a debate that has been likened to a mini-constitutional convention. At issue was this question: Since a president requires the consent of the Senate to appoint certain officials, does he require consent of the Senate to remove them? The Constitution does not explicitly vest authority of removal in a president, and some members of Congress maintained that removal of such officials requires Senate acquiescence. But, under the leadership of James Madison, the House of Representatives recognized a unilateral right of removal, in part from the conviction that "mingling of the powers of the President and Senate" is an "unchaste connexion."

Senators proved more resistant, though that recalcitrance put them in the unenviable position of appearing to distrust the revered patriot. Oliver Ellsworth said that if Washington were deprived of the power of removal, "we may as well lay the President's head on a block and strike it off with a blow." With that declamation, he put a green handkerchief to his face, and, an observer recorded, "either shed tears, or affected to do so." Ellsworth reasoned: "I buy a square acre of land. I buy the trees, waters, and everything belonging to it. The executive power belongs to the President. The removing of officers is a tree on this acre. The power of removing it is, therefore, his. It is in him. It is nowhere else." Despite this oration, the Senate split evenly, and it required the tie-breaking vote of the vice president to carry the day for the president. (Adams went on to resolve twenty-seven more ties, a record that no vice president has ever matched.)

Vesting this authority in the president had momentous consequences for the evolution of the office because, without unhampered power of removal, the chief executive could not put his stamp on his administration. If he had been required to seek permission of the Senate to dismiss subordinates who were incompetent or who undercut his policies, he would not have been able, as Madison pointed out, to fulfill his obligation faithfully to execute the laws. Congress, though, was never altogether reconciled to this "decision of 1789," and it would revisit the question under future presidencies, as Andrew Jackson, Andrew Johnson, and Franklin D. Roosevelt would learn to their sorrow.

In choosing officials to head the three departments Congress created in 1789 (State, Treasury, and War) and in making other important appointments, Washington bore in mind past service to the Patriot cause. He named the principal author of the Declaration of Independence, Thomas Jefferson, as secretary of state, the top place in the administration. For secretary of the treasury, which turned out to be the dynamo of policymaking in his administration, the president chose Alexander Hamilton, who had led a bayonet charge at Yorktown. He selected for secretary of war his former artillery chief, Henry Knox, who had broken the redcoat siege of Boston by hauling sixty tons of cannon more than three hundred miles to Dorchester Heights in the dead of icy winter.

Washington also aimed to be inclusive, with representatives from every section—New England, Middle States, South—because he recognized that there was still considerable distrust of centralized government. Jefferson was a fellow Virginian. Hamilton was a New Yorker, as was John Jay, the most distinguished lawyer in the state, who became Chief Justice of the United States. Knox, who had run a Boston bookshop, was a New Englander.

Washington had other precepts, too. He sought "First Characters," men "who by virtue of their abilities and records of public service stood first . . . in the respect of their neighbors." He denied any place in the government to activists who had been outspoken foes of ratification of the Constitution. Determined to win confidence in the untried government by exhibiting "utmost impartiality," he refused to be swayed by "blood or friendship," even rejecting the plea of his nephew Bushrod for a government post. He told his nephew bluntly, "Your standing at the bar would not justify my nomination of you."

No appointment that Washington made had such huge consequences as that of his choice for secretary of the treasury. Alexander Hamilton was the son of an ill-reputed mother, said to be promiscuous, and a shiftless Scot. Born on Nevis, Hamilton settled with his mother at a young age on another Caribbean island, St. Croix, where, as a teenager, he impressed prominent men with his business acumen. They got up a purse to send him to New York, where he enrolled at King's College. A precocious undergraduate, Hamilton won fame as a Revolutionary pamphleteer and then distinguished himself as an officer in the Patriot army. At Monmouth, his horse was shot out from under him, and at Yorktown he earned Washington's praise for his courage. (Washington, Hamilton said in explaining his meteoric rise to prominence, was "an Aegis very essential" to him.) Voracious for social advancement, Hamilton sought a wife who was "well bred" ("a little learning will do") and carried a "fortune, the larger stock of that the better." He achieved that goal by marrying into New York's elite Schuyler family.

Though no one could question Hamilton's skills, Congress viewed him warily, because it was unwilling to surrender the power of the purse for which colonial legislatures had fought so strenuously. It was fearful that the secretary of the treasury might strive to become a chancellor of the exchequer or even prime minister. Hence, it put him on a different footing from other officials. Unlike the secretaries of state and war, who were under the exclusive jurisdiction of the president, the secretary of the treasury was also answerable to Congress.

Despite these constrictions, the Treasury rapidly became the big gorilla of the new government. Since Congress refused to expand the national government further by creating a home office in the British style, the Treasury, in addition to its immense fiscal responsibilities, was assigned a range of operations from the Customs Service to the Revenue Cutter Service (subsequently the US Coast Guard). "The importance of the Treasury," the scholar Leonard White has pointed out, derived, too, "from the character of its constituency." Through the many agencies Hamilton supervised, he affected a wide range of interests in the country. Hamilton had a staff in the capital of twenty-seven—larger than that of the other department heads combined. With a huge field retinue, he oversaw many hundreds of employees, in contrast to the grand total of twenty-two in the other departments. His staff was bigger even than the president's.

The rest of the government operated on a much smaller scale. Jefferson at State made do with a staff of six, four of them clerks, and the entire diplomatic corps consisted of just two ministers—at Paris and London—with lesser representatives in Madrid, Lisbon, The Hague, and Morocco. The secretary of war began with only three clerks, which may have been all he needed to supervise an army of perhaps five thousand men. The attorney general was a part-time official working on an annual retainer while he carried on his private law practice, so the federal government was only one of his clients. Washington's choice for attorney general, Edmund Randolph, reported, "I am a sort of mongrel here." He supervised no one (the Department of Justice would not be created until 1870), and he did not merit even one clerk. The postmaster general, who did not have departmental status and did not report to the president, performed all his duties in two rooms of his home with two employees. The president of the United States of America had a staff of one.

George Washington, though, demonstrated that he did not require an entourage, for he was a man born to command. The Constitution does not specify that the president is in control of the departments or that employees in the executive branch are his subordinates, and his role could conceivably have been largely ceremonial. But Washington made clear that he was in charge. He had many hundreds of offices to fill, and he did so diligently. "No collector of customs, captain of a cutter, keeper of a lighthouse, or surveyor of revenue was appointed except after specific consideration by the President," Leonard White wrote. Washington also took advantage of his power of removal to discharge seventeen officials who had been appointed with the consent of the Senate, thereby building a body of precedent. Nothing Washington did in his eight years in office was more important than the emphatic manner in which he established that, no doubt about it, the president is chief executive, sole head of the executive branch.

President Washington determined to be a hands-on administrator. He told Jefferson: "I consider the successful Administration of the general Government as an object of almost infinite consequence to the present and future happiness of the Citizens of the United States." Department heads were given to understand that every letter they received had to be submitted to the president for his review. They had "the trouble of making up, once a day, a packet of all their communications for the perusal of the President," Secretary Jefferson reported. Jefferson added:

> If an answer was requisite, the Secretary of the department communicated the letter & his proposed answer to the President. . . . Sometimes he returned them with an informal note, suggesting an alteration or a query. If a doubt of any importance arose, he reserved it for conference. By this means, he was always in accurate possession of all facts & proceedings in every part of the Union, & to whatsoever department they related; he formed a central point for the different branches . . . and met himself the due responsibility for whatever was done.

In his first years, Washington met his chief ministers individually, sometimes at breakfast, but by the end of 1791 he had started to call together the three department heads and the attorney general, and during his second term that practice became customary. In 1793, Madison began to refer to the group as a "cabinet," an institution not provided for in the Constitution. George Washington, the historian Glenn Phelps has written, "continued to act as a founder long after the adjournment of the Philadelphia convention."

❧

Secretary Hamilton, while recognizing a broad range of presidential authority, articulated an expansive vision of America's future. "I

anticipate . . . that the Country will, erelong, assume an attitude cor-
respondent with its great destinies—majestic, efficient, and operative
of great things. A noble carreer lies before it." His object, the historian
John Ferling has pointed out, "was nothing less than the creation of
a modern nation-state, one that was erected on a superstructure that
would equip it to play as an equal on the world stage." In response
to a request from Congress, Hamilton composed a Report on Public
Credit that advocated widening the scope of the central government
by assuming the states' Revolutionary War debts and funding them.
By this step, he believed, he would gain respect for the new country
in the world's financial markets, give budding capitalists a stake in the
constitutional order, and start the United States on its way toward becoming a commercial society. As his astute biographer, Ron Chernow,
has written, "He was the messenger from a future we now inhabit."

Hamilton's ambitions appalled Secretary of State Thomas Jefferson,
who warned Washington that, in undoing the Revolution, they constituted a peril to the republic. Secretary Jefferson wrote to Thomas Paine,
"We have a sect . . . panting after an English constitution of kings, lords,
& commons, & whose heads are itching for crowns, coronets & mitres."
Jefferson believed that Hamilton "was not only a monarchist, but for a
monarchy bottomed on corruption," a blackguard who was creating a
"money phalanx" in the interests of wealthy Northern financiers that
would debase Congress, obliterate states' rights, and end all hope that
America might become an agrarian utopia. Washington, though, could
not be convinced that Hamilton was an evil schemer. He counted himself fortunate to have such an able lieutenant in charge of finances.

Secretary of Treasury Hamilton's initiative for the assumption of
state debts, however, drew numbers of Americans into Secretary
Jefferson's camp. Soldiers of the American Revolution had been paid
in chits that, out of desperation in hard times, they had sold to speculators, and it seemed manifestly unfair to redeem this paper at full
value in large part to the benefit of what Jefferson thought of as "the
stock-jobbing herd." Furthermore, assumption created bitter sectional
animosity. Southern states such as Virginia had taxed themselves to

pay off all or most of their war debts. "Why," asked a Richmond publication, "should Virginians be taxed . . . to help discharge the obligations of Connecticut or Massachusetts?"

For nearly two centuries, historians have explained how the conflict got resolved by relying on Jefferson's recollection of a chance encounter. "Hamilton was in despair," the secretary of state recorded. "He painted pathetically . . . the danger of secession" and sought support from enough Republicans to carry assumption through the House. Jefferson responded, according to his tale, by hosting a dinner at his home on Maiden Lane attended by Hamilton and Madison, a powerful figure in the House, at which a deal was struck. More recently, scholars have expressed skepticism about this narrative. But however the denouement came about, the ensuing events echoed Jefferson's rendering. Though Madison continued in opposition, he lowered his voice, and enough of his followers switched their votes to give Hamilton a triumph for assumption in the House; the South got a dram of satisfaction by a decision to locate the permanent site of the nation's capital along the Potomac, though that would take place only after a decade in Philadelphia. Washington endorsed both features: assumption and the location of the capital at a site that the president chose near Mount Vernon, though that decision evoked some growling about indulgence in self-interest. Jefferson had brooded about the unfairness of assumption, but he wound up concluding that assumption was essential, for if the moneylenders in Amsterdam thought that America was financially irresponsible and denied credit, survival of the republic would be in jeopardy.

The conflict between the president's appointees came to a head over Hamilton's proposal to create a Bank of the United States, which would be the repository of government funds, could issue notes that would be the new nation's currency, and would provide a source of cash for the government at times of financial stringency, but, despite its official provenance, was to be a private corporation with a twenty-year charter. As Hamilton drafted the bill, he had at his hand a copy of the charter of the Bank of England, a provocation to those with vivid memories of the Patriot revolt. Jefferson, who had no understanding of banking and who, as a planter, valued the acquisition of land but not the issue of paper, was so divorced from reality that he thought those engaged in the legerdemain of dispensing currency should be "adjudged guilty of high treason and suffer death."

When Washington confronted the question of whether to sign the bill creating the Bank, he appeared to be so disconcerted by the objections raised not only by Jefferson but by Attorney General Randolph in his administration and by James Madison in the House that he went so far as to ask Madison to draft a veto message for his consideration. At the president's request, Hamilton prepared a lengthy rejoinder, one of a number of powerful documents he crafted. Just two days after Hamilton submitted his elaborate retort, Washington announced his support of the project, which he probably was already inclined to do. The president felt fully justified when on the first day of subscription for the Bank every one of the 20,000 shares was snapped up. "Our public credit," he rejoiced, "stands on ground which three years ago would have been considered as a species of madness to have foretold." (Washington did, however, balk at Hamilton's insistence on fostering factories, a recommendation of his Report on the Subject of Manufactures, in which Hamilton noted approvingly that more than half of the workforce of British cotton mills were women and children, "many of them of a very tender age.")

The dispute over the Bank bill brought about a meaningful dialogue over interpretation of the nation's charter. Madison and Jefferson maintained that nowhere in the Constitution was there a clause authorizing Congress to set up a bank. Hamilton's bill, said Madison, "was condemned by the silence of the Constitution." Virginians and other Southerners were alarmed not only by the prospect of a financial colossus, but also by the realization that, if the national government was conceded the authority to create a bank, it would have free rein to stamp out slavery. Jefferson warned that, in accord with the Tenth Amendment's limitation of national authority, advancing "a single step beyond the boundaries . . . specially drawn around the powers of Congress is to take possession of a boundless field of power, no longer susceptible of any definition." Jefferson's exegesis, Hamilton protested, was framed in a way that partook "of asperity and ill humor towards me."

Hamilton countered this strict constructionist view by producing a document of more than 13,000 words contending that the "necessary and proper" clause of the Constitution implied powers which validated the action—a broad interpretation that the president found persuasive. Especially effective was a citation by a Hamilton supporter from *Federalist 44*: "No axiom is more clearly established in law, or in reason, than that ... wherever a general power to do a thing is given, every particular power necessary for doing it, is included," a sentence written by Hamilton's Bank bill foe, James Madison. This conception of the Constitution had a momentous long-term effect, for it greatly magnified the realm of government under a president's leadership. Late in the twentieth century, in the era of the Great Society, the political scientist Clinton Rossiter asserted that Hamilton's "works and words have been more consequential than those of any other American in shaping the Constitution under which we live."

⟫⟪

Even some critics of centralized power acknowledged that foreign affairs gave Washington a great range of opportunities for vigorous assertion of his authority. Without seeking Senate approval, he employed personal agents, one of them Gouverneur Morris, to conduct diplomatic negotiations in London, Madrid, and Lisbon. He also significantly amplified the meaning of the provision in the Constitution authorizing the president to "receive" ambassadors, a word that suggests a clerk-like function, by claiming for his office the sole right to recognize (or refuse to recognize) foreign governments.

Against the wishes of Hamilton, and without consulting the Senate, Washington decided to receive an emissary from the revolutionary French republic, Edmond-Charles-Edouard Genet, who, in the spirit of the French revolt of 1789, styled himself Citizen Genet. Charleston had cheered Genet when he landed there, and the governor of South Carolina had encouraged him to arm and commission French privateers to prey upon British ships and to set up courts controlled by the local French consul to approve the seizures of vessels flying the Union Jack. (Eventually, these privateers captured more than eighty British merchant vessels, some of them in US territorial waters.) On a triumphal procession up the coast, the French envoy reached Philadelphia, where a crowd of one thousand sang "La Marseillaise" lustily. "I live in the midst of perpetual festivals," Genet said.

This exuberant reception deprived the envoy of what little common sense he may have had. He fitted out a prize ship, *Little Sarah*, retitled *La Petite Démocrate*, as a privateer in defiance of the American government's desire for neutrality and then, ignoring an explicit order to confine the vessel to harbor, instructed its captain to set sail. Jefferson, who initially was pleased that the enthusiasm for the Frenchman meant that "all the old spirit of 1776 is rekindling," told Madison that Genet had been "disrespectful & even indecent toward the P., . . . talking of appeals from him to Congress, from them to the people." (Genet, he warned indifferent Republican leaders, would "*sink the republican* interest if they do not *abandon him*.") In his role as secretary of state, Jefferson informed Genet sternly that "as the President is the only channel of communication between the United States and foreign nations, it is from him alone that foreign nations or their agents are to learn . . . the will of the nation." Heedless of this admonition, Genet behaved so outrageously— seeking to incite Francophile mobs against the American government and to arm Kentuckians to invade Spanish borderlands—that Washington demanded his recall. (Knowing that his most likely destination at home was the guillotine, for he had been excoriated by Robespierre, Genet chose to repatriate, marrying the daughter of the governor of New York and assuming the identity of a Hudson Valley squire.)

European conflicts, important though they were, did not require nearly so much of Washington's attention to diplomacy as dealings with Indian nations, and those negotiations would, in turn, impinge on the president's relations with both houses of Congress, sometimes in unexpected ways. No Continental envoy was treated to the sump-tuous feasts laid on by the president for the Creek leader Alexander McGillivray and more than two dozen other chiefs, who, at the end of this courtship, put their marks on a treaty of New York spelling out their territorial claims. (McGillivray was the son of a Scot father and of a mother born to a French man and a Native American woman.) To solemnize this pact, Washington issued an executive order, the Proclamation of 1790, banning encroachments on Indian lands. Unhappily, one of the many legacies Washington left his successors was the pattern of his subsequent performance: good intentions, awful results. History, he acknowledged, would not be fair to Indians: "They, poor wretches, have no Press thro' which their grievances are related; and . . . when one side only of a Story is heard, and often repeated, the human mind becomes impressed with it, insensibly."

Though Washington thought that native uprisings were largely the fault of covetous whites, he sent armed forces to suppress them, in good part because he sought to bind frontier settlers to the union. One of these expeditions, led by Major General Arthur St. Clair in the Old Northwest, had the order: "Seek the enemy and endeavor by all possible means to strike them with great severity." Jefferson, who had written memorably that all men were created equal, told Washington, "I hope we shall give the Indians a thorough drubbing." Instead, the Miami ambushed St. Clair's invaders, killing more than half of the soldiers and destroying all the supplies. A congressman called the rout "the most complete victory ever known in this country obtained by Indians." The defeat also nearly precipitated a constitutional crisis.

✦✦

In 1792, Washington skated to the edge of asserting executive privilege when the House of Representatives demanded documents pertaining to the St. Clair disaster. Reluctant to further an inquiry into an event that embarrassed his administration, Washington brought the question to his cabinet, saying that it was vital to make the correct response be-cause it could set a precedent. The cabinet reasoned that there would be no harm in this instance in complying, and Washington agreed to capitulate. (Two years later, he confronted a request to turn over to the Senate correspondence of the US minister to France, the ubiquitous Gouverneur Morris, who had made derogatory comments about French leaders. Washington transmitted the letters, "except in those particulars, in my judgment, for public considerations, ought not be communicated," and the Senate did not challenge his right to withhold these items. So, for the first time, a president won acceptance of a claim to executive privilege, though only to a modest extent.)

Washington behaved prudently because, though he would not permit any infringement upon his prerogatives, he respected the authority of Congress. In eight years, he vetoed just two bills, both times hesitantly. He made no use of the power at all until the spring of 1792, when he vetoed a bill apportioning members of the House of Representatives, and then only because Jefferson warned him that if he did not, the right to veto would atrophy. Furthermore, the measure was flagrantly unconstitutional. A president, Washington believed, should not employ the veto in order to impede legislation he disliked, but only if it transgressed the Constitution. He departed from that stance just once—on national security grounds when, as his tenure was drawing to a close, Congress voted to eliminate two companies of dragoons that he judged necessary to safeguard the western frontier. "What sets Washington apart," Glenn Phelps has written, "is his willingness to cooperate whenever possible with Congress. Consultation, not confrontation, characterized his administrative demeanor." At one point, Washington wrote, "Motives of delicacy have uniformly restrained the P—— from introducing any topick which relates to Legislative matters to members . . . of Congress, lest it should be expected that he wished to influence the question before it." Washington did, though, permit Madison to benefit from the president's endorsement to put through ten amendments to the Constitution that became cherished as the Bill of Rights. Washington's reticence had one regrettable feature, however, for he rejected a plea to bring pressure on Congress to curb slavery.

George Washington set one important precedent inadvertently. Since the Constitution stipulates that the president, in negotiating treaties, must seek the "Advice and Consent of the Senate," he entered the US Senate chamber in August 1789 to consult about a pact with Creeks. The legislators, bemused by the expectation of an instant response, fell silent, and then engaged in cacophonous discussion before referring the matter to committee. If one of the senators is to be believed (his reliability has been questioned), Washington "started up in a Violent fret," and said, "This defeats every purpose of my coming here." On his way out, he was reported to have been overheard muttering that he would be damned if he ever went there again. Two days later, he returned, but that was the last time—for him and for his successors. In this manner, in the very first year of the republic, "Advice," insofar as it implied personal consultation, was, in effect, expunged from the Constitution, though presidents have continued to convey information in writing to senators and to acknowledge their role in ratifying treaties.

Over the course of four years, Washington more than fulfilled the high expectations of the American people, and, as the end of his term approached, he requested Madison to prepare a farewell address for him—only to find that he would be granted no surcease because he was needed to heal a grievous breach in his administration. In May 1791, Jefferson and Madison had gone off on a botany excursion that took them as far north as Lake Champlain, a trip that, though they undeniably studied azaleas and blackberry vines and visited hallowed Revolutionary War sites such as Saratoga, has often been viewed as a cover for a scheme to create a political party. In fact, neither man's thinking had reached that point, and both deplored the rise of faction. Jefferson, the historian Joyce Appleby has maintained, fostered "not a party, but a radical political movement, mobilized to save the American Revolution from—excuse the anachronism—its thermidorean reaction."

Yet Jefferson did fear that, because of what he viewed to be Hamilton's scheming, the country was reversing the achievement of the Patriots in the Revolution and "galloping fast into monarchy," and Hamilton, in turn, under the pen name Catullus, called Jefferson an "intriguing incendiary." By 1792, Hamilton and Jefferson were at each other's throats, with Hamilton judging the secretary of state guilty of perpetrating "the most wanton and flagitious actions that ever stained the annals of a civilized nation," and Jefferson urging the poet Philip Freneau, a fierce Anglophobe and hater of the rich, to dip his pen in vitriol. Jefferson gave Freneau a position in his department, which meant that the money of the government would be used to sabotage government policies. Indeed, the headstrong Freneau was soon attacking not only Hamilton but President Washington, whom he accused of "monarchical prettiness." Years later, Jefferson remembered this as a time when he and Hamilton were "daily pitted . . . like two cocks."

Under these circumstances, Washington was persuaded to stay on in the hope that he might bring a halt to "wounding suspicions" and, as he wrote in confidential letters to each man, to "internal dissensions" that were "harrowing and tearing our vitals." He told Jefferson that if his two appointees did not agree to lay "shoulders to the machine after measures are decided on," he foresaw that "the fairest prospect of happiness & prosperity that ever was presented to man will be lost— perhaps for ever!" Hamilton received a similar letter. Neither of the president's subordinates responded reassuringly, though Jefferson informed Washington that "North and South will hang together, if they can hang on you," and Hamilton told the president that his departure would be regarded "as the greatest evil that could befall the country at the present juncture." Washington was re-elected by acclamation, with John Adams returned to the vice presidency.

+-+

Washington would have done well to carry out his intention to retire, for his second term, with its unabated partisan bitterness, foreshadowed the difficulties that have so often been the lot of presidents in their second four years. The war between Great Britain and France that erupted in 1793, which would roil American politics for nearly two decades, greatly intensified the rancor. In that conflict, Hamilton sided with the British whom he valued as America's primary trading partner, while Jefferson longed for the day when he could sit down to tea with French generals in London.

This division mirrored their divergence over the French Revolution. Jefferson saw the fall of the Bastille as happy confirmation that the Declaration of Independence he had crafted had initiated a movement toward liberty, equality, and fraternity that was sweeping the world, while Hamilton deplored the social leveling and was shocked by the savage Reign of Terror. The French Revolution, Hamilton later said, "has been always to me an object of horror." He accused Madison as well as Jefferson of having "a womanish attachment to France and a womanish resentment against Great Britain." In contrast, Jefferson wrote to a former private secretary who had turned against the Revolution, "Was ever such a prize won with so little innocent blood? My own affections have been deeply wounded by some of the martyrs to this cause, but rather than it should have failed, I would have seen half the earth desolated. Were there but an Adam & Eve left in every country, & left free, it would be better than as it now is."

War between France and Britain gave Washington an ample field to assert his authority but challenged him to find an appropriate stance. He acknowledged the debt owed to Rochambeau's soldiers and de Grasse's sailors at Yorktown, and he was moved when Lafayette sent him the key to the Bastille. He recognized, too, that American citizens were joyfully dancing La Carmagnole and sporting cockades. On early morning walks in Philadelphia, he saw tricolors displayed in windows. Moreover, the alliance negotiated during the American Revolution committed his country to go to the aid of the French if they were attacked. But Washington feared that if Americans actively supported the French, the British would take up arms against the former colonials and crush the republic in its infancy.

In mid-April 1793, the president asked his cabinet whether he should issue a declaration of neutrality. All four members agreed that neutrality was imperative, but Jefferson objected that a neutrality statement was equivalent to determining that there should not be war, and Congress had sole constitutional authority to decide on war. Furthermore, a premature declaration would deprive America of its bargaining leverage with the two countries, for such an announcement could be "a thing worth something to the powers at war . . . and we might reasonably ask as a price the *broadest privileges* of neutral nations." Consequently, when Washington issued a proclamation on April 22, he omitted the word "neutrality," contenting himself with announcing America's determination to pursue "a conduct friendly and impartial to the belligerent powers" and prohibiting Americans from "committing, aiding, or abetting hostilities against any of the said powers or . . . carrying to them . . . contraband." The president reasoned that the alliance with France had been made with the king, who had been dethroned, and so was no longer binding, but he stopped short of formally terminating it.

The proclamation touched off a fierce debate over the meaning of the Constitution between two of the early prominent leaders who had been allied as the principal authors of *The Federalist*. Hamilton precipitated the controversy by asserting in a series of newspaper articles under the pseudonym Pacificus (Lover of Peace) that control of foreign affairs was "inherently" the prerogative of the president, who had discretionary authority that was not cabined by any power granted to Congress. Madison, though, was implored by Jefferson, "For God sakes my dear Sir, take up your pen, select the most striking heresies and cut him to pieces." Under the pseudonym Helvidius (Lover of Liberty), Madison charged that Hamilton's claim for a freewheeling executive was "in theory an absurdity—in practice a tyranny," a "vicious" doctrine borrowed from the British crown. Madison maintained that Congress alone had the power to declare war, form alliances, or proclaim neutrality and that the president was merely an administrator of policies set by the legislative branch.

The "Neutrality Proclamation," as it became called despite Washington's discreet wording, intensified political polarization. "The cause of France is the cause of man," said a Jeffersonian leader in Pennsylvania, "and neutrality is desertion." Not even the president was spared. "Ten thousand people in the streets in Philadelphia, day after day, threatened to drag Washington out of his house and effect a revolution in the government, or compel it to declare in favour of the French Revolution and against England," wrote John Adams. "And thus," observed his son, John Quincy Adams, "the party movements in our own country became complicated with the sweeping hurricane of European politics and war."

At the end of 1793, Jefferson resigned as secretary of state, "with the longing of a wave-worn mariner, who has at length the land in view," and Washington named a longtime ally, the tidewater patrician Edmund Randolph, to succeed him, a decision he came to regret. Washington later compelled Randolph's resignation after angrily confronting him with a dispatch to a French official that had been intercepted by a British warship. The letter could be read to imply that the new secretary of state was willing to advocate a pro-French foreign policy in return for a bribe. The president first learned of this incident after Timothy Pickering, who had succeeded Knox as secretary of war, beseeched him to return from a short stay in Mount Vernon to go to the capital "for a *special reason* which can be communicated to you only in private." At the executive mansion, Pickering, pointing toward the room in which Randolph was seated, told Washington, "That man is a traitor!" Randolph stoutly denied the charge, and scholars find the evidence inconclusive, while expressing contempt for Pickering. After being subjected to intense interrogation, Randolph, saying he would not stay on after such treatment, resigned his post as secretary of state.

Jefferson retired to Virginia, where he claimed to be forever rooted, as an Antediluvian patriarch "enjoying at home peace, peaches, and poplars," but it did not take long for him to rouse himself for combat. Together with Madison, he encouraged the creation of a Democratic-Republican Party, soon called the Republican Party (no relation to the later organization of that name). The Hamilton faction responded by setting up a Federalist Party, which championed the policies of the Washington administration. Though the Republicans spoke the rhetoric of the French Revolution, their stronghold was the South of slave plantations. In part for that reason, they gave priority to states' rights. The Federalists favored a powerful executive branch in a strong national government, wanted to enlarge the peacetime army, sought to foster commerce, preferred Britain to France, and had a more pronounced inclination toward a hierarchical social order. "There must be," a Federalist averred, "rulers and subjects, masters and servants, rich and poor." A prominent party leader, Fisher Ames, claimed that Federalists were "the wise, and good, and rich." The Federalist bastion was mercantile and maritime New England with its large stake in trading with Britain and its Caribbean colonies.

The president, while abhorring the notion of political parties, became, in truth, the leader of the Federalists in his second term. Increasingly, he distributed patronage for partisan purposes. "I shall not, whilst I have the honour to administer the government, bring a man into any office of consequence knowingly, whose political tenets are adverse to the measures which the general government [is] pursuing; for this, in my opinion, would be a sort of political suicide," he said. Everyone in his final cabinet identified himself with the Federalists.

George Washington further exacerbated partisan divisions by approving a tax promoted by Hamilton that triggered the most dramatic episode of his presidency. An excise on whiskey fell brutally on frontier farmers, far from markets, who lowered transportation costs for their corn and rye by shipping their grains in the form of distilled liquor. Whiskey was essential, too, for recruiting farm laborers, who required liberal rations of hard stuff as inducements. Hamilton himself had remarked in *The Federalist* that Americans would "ill brook" excise taxes.

In four western Pennsylvania counties, farmers resisted, passively at first, then, in the summer of 1794, violently. They tarred and feathered tax collectors, expelled a federal marshal, robbed the mail, forced the surrender of a US army contingent, torched the home of a revenue inspector, and, by the thousands, marched on Pittsburgh brandishing weapons. These actions greatly disturbed Washington, who had long thought that control of the back country was essential to the security of the republic. He had also bought many thousands of acres on the frontier and as a consequence had a large stake in its success.

Hamilton regarded the uprising as not merely unlawful but treasonous, and Washington, while not so persuaded, issued a proclamation ordering the "insurgents to disperse and retire peaceably to their respective abodes," though he also sought reconciliation. Alarmed that the authority of the American government was being flouted and fearful that the dissidents, who approached both Britain and Spain, might align with a foreign power, the president sought a writ from a US Supreme Court justice. That exponent of presidential prerogatives at the constitutional convention, James Wilson, who had been elevated to the Court, obliged by certifying that the laws of the land were being disregarded "by combinations too powerful to be suppressed by the ordinary course of judicial proceedings." Fortified by this writ, Washington called upon the governors of four states to provide militia to quell the protesters.

After the states mobilized nearly thirteen thousand soldiers, Washington, taking literally his designation in the Constitution as commander in chief, traveled to Carlisle, Pennsylvania, where, in the blue-and-buff uniform of the Patriot army, he inspected the troops— a force five times larger than he had led into battle at Trenton in the Revolutionary War. His presence had a reassuring effect. A Pennsylvania soldier reported that "THE MAN OF THE PEOPLE, with a mien intrepid as that of Hector, yet graceful as that of Paris, moved slowly onward." After the president returned to Philadelphia, Hamilton, saying that every rebel should be "skewered, shot, or hanged on the first tree," rode a gray charger as one of the heads of an armed force into western Pennsylvania, where it met no resistance. The uprising, which was never remotely treasonous, melted away. Small numbers of men were arrested; most were not tried; and only two were convicted. They were sentenced to death, but Washington, drawing on another of his constitutional powers, pardoned them.

By his bold moves, especially by his theatrical journey, Washington demonstrated that he was fully prepared to "take Care that the Laws be faithfully executed." Because he was held in such high esteem, he succeeded in getting Pennsylvania militia to put down their fellow citizens in order to uphold the authority of an untried government that had imposed a hated tax. And in sustaining the supremacy of the national government, he had also underscored the power of the presidency.

Not everyone applauded his behavior, however, especially after he denounced democratic societies that had supported the beleaguered farmers—a chiding that Madison viewed as undermining First Amendment freedom of expression. Critics muttered that Washington had been imposed upon by Hamilton to inflate a protest into a mutiny and to respond with overkill. A year earlier, Jefferson had warned Washington that Hamilton aimed "to dismount him from the head of the nation." The government's response to the Whiskey Rebellion, Madison concluded, was a scheme "to connect the Democratic Societies with odium of the insurrection—to connect the Republicans in Congress with those societies—to put the President ostensibly at the head of the other party."

⊁⊰

While seeking to preserve domestic tranquility, Washington also had to cope with the travail of the European conflict, and that task, too, had political repercussions. A British Order in Council that led to the seizure or confiscation of hundreds of US merchant vessels in the French West Indies trade quickened a drumbeat for war, and Washington strengthened US defenses by ordering construction of six frigates, giving birth to the United States Navy. But the president, realizing that America was grievously unprepared for combat with the mightiest sea power, chose the path of negotiation by sending Chief Justice Jay to London in 1794 as envoy plenipotentiary. Washington never accepted the judiciary as a separate branch, in accordance with the rubric of separation of powers, but thought of the justices as members of the national government he headed. He once even asked the Court for an advisory opinion, only to be rebuked. Despite this scolding, he did not hesitate to enlist the chief justice in a policy assignment.

Despite bargaining from a position of weakness since Britannia ruled the waves, Jay did not come away empty-handed, though he did not get much. The British agreed to vacate posts in the area northwest of the original thirteen colonies (that they had already pledged to do in the 1783 treaty) and, with the redcoats gone, and Indians dispersed by General Anthony Wayne at the Battle of Fallen Timbers, new American communities arose: Cleveland, Dayton, Youngstown. The British also consented to pay for spoliations on US commerce and to give the United States certain paltry trading privileges in the West Indies, which both Washington and the Senate found humiliating. Jay, in return, agreed to write into the treaty London's conception of maritime law and to deny the United States the practice of re-exporting cotton. He acknowledged, too, that American debtors, primarily Virginia planters, needed to meet their long-standing obligations to British creditors. The pact also stipulated that British privateers could enter US harbors (though French privateers could not.) Britain continued to insist on its right to board US ships, seize sailors, and impress them in its navy. It refused to pledge that it would cease arming Indians.

Washington, after initial misgivings, made the difficult decision to accept the treaty because it avoided war. For all its shortcomings, Jay's Treaty served American interests well. In particular, US commerce with its foremost trading partner boomed, and customs receipts were an indispensable asset to the young government. In sum, Joseph Ellis has elucidated, Jay's Treaty "bet, in effect, on England rather than France as the hegemonic European power of the future, which proved prophetic." It thereby rejected, he added, "the Jeffersonian presumption that England was . . . on the downward slope of history."

The president's decision to sign the treaty evoked fierce domestic discontent. It had arisen even before the terms of the pact were known, on the assumption that Britain was determined to subject the United States to colonial status, obliterating the achievement of the Patriots.

Jefferson called the agreement negotiated by Jay "really nothing more than a treaty of alliance between England & the Anglomen of this country against the legislature & people of the United States," and his fellow Republicans deplored the Jay mission for enlarging executive power. The president, charged the foremost Republican journal, had behaved "as if he were the omnipotent director of a seraglio." Jay said that he could have walked at night the length of the Atlantic seaboard by the light of fires burning him in effigy, and when, at a gathering in New York City, Hamilton sought to defend the pact, he was pelted with stones. An opponent in New York posted graffiti: "Damn John Jay! Damn everyone who won't damn John Jay!! Damn everyone who won't put lights in the windows and sit up all night damning John Jay!!!" Southerners especially resented the refusal by Jay, a foe of slavery, to pursue avidly their demand for reparations for the loss of slaves seized by redcoats in the Revolution. Fury at Jay's Treaty drove a number of the president's most ardent admirers into the ranks of Republican critics of his administration. Once the Senate ratified the treaty (barely reaching the required two-thirds), Washington never spoke to Jefferson again.

In 1796, the House of Representatives, hoping to expose wrongdoing by the Federalists, called on the president to transmit the administration's papers on the negotiation of Jay's Treaty. This demand raised two fundamental questions. Did a pact negotiated by a president require the consent not only of the Senate, as the Constitution specified, but also of the House, which could deny appropriations for implementing a treaty? Could a president refuse to submit documents because, in his judgment, compliance would jeopardize national security? Washington left no doubt of his answers. The papers, he replied, were not relevant "to any purpose under the cognizance of the House of Representatives, except that of an impeachment, which the resolution has not expressed." Moreover, "the nature of foreign negotiations requires caution." Hence full disclosure was contrary to the national interest. In sum, he wrote, "a just regard to the constitution and to the duty of my office . . . forbids a compliance with your request."

The president reminded the House that "having been a member of the general convention and knowing the principles on which the constitution was formed," he was fully apprised that the treaty-making power was assigned exclusively to the president and the Senate.

Sullenly, a closely divided House, spurred by Madison, persisted. Called upon to vote on an appropriation to finance provisions of the treaty, it split 49–49, placing the outcome in the hands of the chair of the Committee of the Whole, Frederick Muhlenberg. He was an ardent Jeffersonian Republican, but he was told by a pro-treaty Pennsylvanian that if "you do not give us your vote, your son shall not have my Polly." Muhlenberg's vote in favor of the treaty left his career in ashes. So frenzied was pro-French allegiance that he did not dare offer himself for re-election. In addition, his brother-in-law, a committed Republican, stabbed him for his alliance with the Federalists. With the House called upon to vote again, at a time when public sentiment was shifting in favor of the treaty, since it avoided war, the House consented to the appropriation. (At about the same time as this triumph, Washington scored another victory when Pinckney's Treaty—the Treaty of San Lorenzo—accorded the United States unimpeded navigation of the Mississippi in a pact with Spain.)

As memories of the general's steadfast courage at Valley Forge and the triumph at Yorktown receded, however, journalists and politicians felt much less reticence about savaging George Washington, though he continued to be widely admired. A Republican wrote, "If ever a nation was debauched by a man, the American nation has been debauched by WASHINGTON." A particularly vicious critic accused the president of "stately journeying through the American continent in search of personal incense," and another writer charged the president with "political degeneracy." A cartoonist even depicted the president's head, bearing a crown, beneath the blade of a guillotine. In an open letter to Washington, the famed Revolutionary-era pamphleteer Thomas Paine charged, "You slept away your time in the field," concluding, "As to you, sir, treacherous in private friendship (for so you have been to me, and that in the day of danger) and a hypocrite in public life, the world will be puzzled to decide whether you are an apostate or an imposter; whether you have abandoned good principles, or whether you ever had any." Jefferson went so far as to confide that a line from Joseph Addison's drama *Cato* might be pertinent for Washington: "Curse on his virtues, they have undone his country." In a letter to Philip Mazzei, which his Italian friend later turned over to a Florentine newspaper, Jefferson was understood to be alluding to Washington when he referred to "men who were Samsons in the field and Solomons in the council, but who have had their heads shorn by the harlot England."

➻➻

As the 1796 election approached, admirers pressed Washington to agree to continue in office, but once again he declined, and this time he could not be dissuaded. He was unwilling to absorb anymore being reviled "in the public prints by a set of infamous scribblers," he said, "in such . . . indecent terms as could scarcely be applied to a Nero, to a notorious defaulter, or even to a common pickpocket." After a cabinet meeting at which Washington was informed that he was the object of yet another dreadful verbal assault, Jefferson recorded: "The Presidt was much inflamed, got into one of those passions when he cannot command himself. . . . Defied any man on earth to produce one single act of his since he had been in the government which was not done on the purest motives. That he had never repented but once . . . having slipped the moment of resigning his office, and that was every moment since. That *by god* he had rather be in his grave than in his present situation." In stepping down, Washington had no intention of decreeing a two-term limit, but he did demonstrate, for a final time, his willingness to relinquish power, and any successor who contemplated a third term had to recognize that he would be measured by the first president's example.

The country learned of his resolve when in September 1796 Washington presented his Farewell Address, to which Hamilton contributed. Despite its title, the "Address" was not an oration but an essay published in a newspaper and republished by many others. In this valedictory, Washington added another component to the role of an American president that many of his successors would copy: lay preacher to the people. Speaking as "a parting friend," he stressed the need for national unity. He warned sternly, too, against "foreign entanglements," an admonition later misconstrued as a plea for perdurable isolationism. In fact, he was calling attention to the particular peril faced by a republic in its first years if its citizens allied themselves with foreign powers. "With me," Washington explained, "a predominant motive has been to endeavor to gain time to our country to settle & mature." He also sought to instruct Americans in Realpolitik. "There can be no greater error than to . . . calculate upon real favours from Nation to Nation," he advised. "'Tis an illusion which experience must cure, which a just pride ought to discard." Washington denounced, too, the scourge of party, for "the alternate domination of one faction over the other . . . has perpetuated the most horrid enormities." Washington's testament has become a hallowed document that every February 22 (his birthday) is read in both houses of Congress.

In treating party as an evil which "serves always to distract the public councils and enfeeble the public administration," Washington was not introducing a new thought but expressing the convictions of his generation and of ages past. The First Marquis of Halifax in his *Maxims of State* of 1693 had written that "Parties . . . like Freebooters, hang out False Colours; the pretence is the Publick Good; the real Business is to catch Prizes; like the Tartars, where-ever they succeed, instead of improving their Victory, they presently fall upon the Baggage." The Federalist John Adams thought "the division of the Republic into two great Parties . . . the greatest political Evil under our Constitution," and in 1798 Jefferson, though by then a partisan, said, "If I could not go to heaven but with a party, I would not go there at all."

Political parties continued to flourish, however. Neither of the factions that arose in these years foresaw the emergence of a two-party system (and the impact it would have on democratic polity and the election of the president). Both thought of their organizations as emergency makeshifts, and they regarded their opponents as illegitimate. Republicans justified their coalition as a temporary departure from virtuous government necessitated by the imperative to thwart the achievements of the Patriots, while the Federalists thought they were defending the government against Jacobin incendiaries. Yet by the end of Washington's tenure, congressmen, who had started out living in boardinghouses with members from their own states, bedded down instead in Republican or Federalist abodes, and few thought it odd that in 1796 voters confronted a choice between just two candidates, each sponsored by a party.

The system for choosing a president was still primitive. Neither the Federalist candidate, John Adams, nor the Republican choice, Thomas Jefferson, campaigned, and neither party offered a platform. Despite his gravitation toward the Federalists, Washington, in keeping with his Bolingbroke style, made no attempt to influence voters on behalf of the man who had served as his vice president for eight years. Furthermore, only a small proportion of the population could vote. Property requirements restricted male suffrage; slaves had no civil rights; and women continued to be political outcasts. Only six of the sixteen states provided solely for popular participation in the choice of electors; in seven, the legislature decided, and three used mixed systems. In such circumstances, it was difficult to forecast a winner, but Adams liked his chances. He told his wife, "I am Heir Apparent you know."

When the 1796 electoral vote was tallied, it fell to Adams, as presiding officer of the Senate, to announce the name of the winner: John Adams. That was not the only curious aspect of the outcome. Jefferson, as the runner-up, though by only three electoral votes, became vice president—with the odd result that the country found itself with a president from one party and a vice president of the opposing party. However rudimentary the system, the country came through its first contested race peacefully, the losers giving no thought to challenging the outcome. Indeed, when Jefferson heard that the contest was likely to end in a tie, he prodded Madison to make sure that the victor would be Adams, "who has always been my senior from the commencement of our public life." Besides, war with France apparently in the offing, Jefferson remarked, "I know well that no man will ever bring out of that office the reputation which carries him into it. . . . This is certainly not a moment to covet the helm." The presidency, he added, "is but a splendid misery."

⊱⊰

The British historian Marcus Cunliffe wrote that "the dying Roman emperor Vespasian is supposed to have murmured: 'Alas, I think I am about to become a god.'. . . George Washington . . . might with justice have thought the same thing as he lay on his deathbed at Mount Vernon in 1799." Americans then, and in generations to come, knew they could count themselves fortunate that, at the very birthing moment of the republic, they had a Periclean leader. When Benjamin Franklin died in the spring of 1790, he left a will providing: "My fine crab-tree walking stick, with a gold head curiously wrought in the form of a cap of liberty, I give to my friend, and the friend of mankind, George Washington. If it were a scepter, he has merited it and would become it." But Washington wanted no imperial rod. "America," Daniel Webster later said, "has furnished to the world the character of Washington, and if our American institutions had done nothing else, that alone would have entitled them to the respect of mankind." The House of Representatives adopted a resolution drafted by a Washington cavalry officer "to the memory of the MAN, first in war, first in peace, and first in the hearts of his countrymen."

When Washington had been sworn into office, he realized that many people in Europe, and not a few in the United States, were watching to see how soon he would be wearing a crown. To the surprise of skeptical observers, especially those in European courts, he betrayed no lust for a prolonged reign. On the day that he surrendered power, the only entry in his diary was, "Much such a day as yesterday in all respects. Mercury at 41." Talleyrand, Napoleon's cynical foreign minister, eventually acknowledged that Washington was "the man who . . . first dared to believe that he could inspire degenerate nations with the courage to rise to the level of republican virtue." On hearing

COMMEMORATION of WASHINGTON.

This 1802 engraving, "Apotheosis of Washington," by John James Barralet reveals the classical iconography that developed after Washington's death, a significant feature of the subsequent glorification of US presidents. *National Portrait Gallery, NPG.2011.138* that Washington, after earlier resigning as commander of the army, was giving up his position as ruler of his country, George III was said to have called the president "the greatest character of the age."

"My political conduct," Washington remarked in 1789, "must be exceedingly circumspect . . . for the eyes of Argus are upon me." Throughout the eight years of his tenure, he respected the limits imposed by the Constitution. When frantic governors asked him for armed forces to repel anticipated Indian attacks, Washington replied that Congress alone had the power to declare war. Though Washington was subject to assaults by the press, he advocated lower postal rates for newspapers. The presidency of George Washington was, as Clinton Rossiter later wrote, "nothing if not painfully constitutional."

For all his reticence, Washington was determined to win the allegiance of the American people to the new government. When he issued his first Thanksgiving Proclamation, he sought a blessing not for the states but for the federal government and the Constitution. (On announcing that proclamation, he also revealed the benign man behind his frosty demeanor by donating beer and food to those imprisoned for debt in the nation's capital.) During a tour of New England, he refused to call upon the governor of Massachusetts, John Hancock, until Hancock first paid him a visit—for he did not want to suggest deference by the head of the national government to a state official. He also refused to set foot in Rhode Island, which had not ratified the Constitution. A year later, with ratification effected, he made the arduous trip north again to pay his respects to the new member of the union, and, after departing, sent a "Letter to the Hebrew Congregation of Newport, Rhode Island" expressing disdain at the notion of toleration, which was patronizing, "for, happily, the Government of the United States . . . gives to bigotry no sanctions, to persecution no assistance." He sent good wishes to "the children of the stock of Abraham" and, borrowing from the Bible (1 Kings 4:25), expressed the aspiration that "every one shall sit in safety under his own vine and figtree and there shall be none to make him afraid."

Every measured assessment of the first president agrees on his greatness. "It seemed to me," wrote Joseph Ellis, "that Benjamin Franklin was

wiser than Washington; Alexander Hamilton was more brilliant; John
Adams was better read; Thomas Jefferson was more intellectually sophis-
ticated; James Madison was more politically astute. Yet each and all of
these prominent figures acknowledged that Washington was their un-
questioned superior." The bracketing of Washington and Franklin, Garry
Wills has commented, "is aptly symbolized by the fact that they (and only
they) achieved a consistent iconography as classical heroes—Cincinnatus
in Washington's case, Prometheus in Franklin's." At the time, Thomas
Jefferson offered a well-rounded appraisal of George Washington:

> His mind was great and powerful, without being of the very first order;
> his penetration strong, tho' not so acute as that of a Newton, Bacon, or
> Locke. . . .
>
> Perhaps the strongest feature in his character was prudence, never
> acting until every . . . consideration was maturely weighed. . . . His in-
> tegrity was most pure. . . . He was indeed, in every sense of the word, a
> wise, a good, & a great man. . . .
>
> His character was . . . perfect . . . never did nature and fortune com-
> bine more perfectly to make a man great.

Jefferson also reflected, "I felt on his death, with my countrymen, that
verily a great man hath fallen in Israel."

By filling in the spaces left by the Framers, George Washington had
a very considerable influence on shaping the institution of the presidency. Washington, the political scientist Michael Riccards pointed
out, "began with a collection of clauses and an unformed office and
crafted them into a constitution." Nearly two centuries later, Leonard
White concluded that "the impact of events and the personality of
Washington on the office had given it living form and substance."
On a chill March day in 1797, ten years after the Framers gathered
in Philadelphia, George Washington was, with no thought of further
glory, surrendering the powers of his office to his successor. When
the transition was completed, a Federalist journal summed up the
thoughts of many: "Thus ended a scene the parallel of which was
never before witnessed in any country."

3

John Adams

Preserving the Republic in Wartime

Called to succeed George Washington, John Adams took on a daunting assignment. He was the first of a number of presidents to labor in the shadow of a larger-than-life predecessor, and none loomed larger than the man who was "first in the hearts of his countrymen." Adams wrote of his inauguration in 1797: "A solemn scene it was indeed, and it was made more affecting to me by the presence of the General, whose Countenance was as serene and unclouded as the day. He Seem'd to enjoy a Tryumph over me. Methought I heard him think 'Ay! I am fairly out and you fairly in! see which of Us will be happiest.'" With characteristic acerbity, Adams wondered whether the tears people shed that day were "from the Loss of their beloved President, or from the Accession of an unbeloved one."

Austere, irascible, petty, John Adams appeared to go out of his way to be unbeloved. "At times," the political scientist Stephen Knott has observed, "it seemed as if Adams believed that successful public service was defined by the number of people one alienated." More than a decade before taking office, he commented, "Popularity was never my Mistress, nor was I ever, or shall I ever be, a popular Man." He added, "But one thing I know, a Man must be Sensible of the errors of the People, and . . . must run the risque of their Displeasure sometimes, or he will never do them any good in the long run." Joseph Ellis characterized the Adams style as "enlightened perversity," which revealed

In this engraving by Amos Doolittle, *A Display of the United States of America*, John Adams is surrounded by the insignia and statistics of the sixteen states. The militant-looking eagle surmounting the composition grasps in its talons a ribbon inscribed with the defiant slogan of 1798: "Millions for our defence, not a cent for tribute." The eagle, however, holds not only an arrow but also an olive branch. Before his term ended, Adams would secure peace with France—his greatest achievement. *Library of Congress, LC-DIG-ppmsca-15716*

itself in "an iconoclastic and contrarian temperament that relished alienation." Adams acknowledged in his diary that he was "puffy, vain, conceited," and that vanity was his "cardinal folly." He admonished himself: "Oh! That I could wear out of my mind every mean and base affection, conquer my natural Pride and Self Conceit, expect no more defference from my fellows than I deserve, acquire that meekness and humility which are the sure marks and Characters of a great and generous Soul."

His pomposity led critics to bestow on the balding, pudgy man with "sesquipedality of belly" the mock honorific, "His Rotundity." If he were painted, Adams remarked, he should be portrayed as "a short thick fat archbishop." He also characterized himself as "a morose Philosopher and a Surly Politician." Adams, reflected Benjamin Franklin, "means well for his Country, is always an honest Man, often a Wise One, but sometimes and in some things, absolutely out of his Senses."

In a letter to James Madison from Paris, Thomas Jefferson offered a more measured view:

> You know the opinion I *formerly* entertained of *my friend Mr. Adams.* Yourself and the governor were the first who *shook* that opinion. I afterwards saw proofs which *convicted* him of a degree of *vanity*, and of *blindness* to it, of which no germ *had appeared* in Congress. A *7-months'* intimacy with him *here* and as many *weeks* in *London* have given me opportunities of studying him closely. *He is vain, irritable and a bad calculator of* the force and probable effect of the motives which govern men. This is *all* the *ill* which can possibly be *said of him.* He is as disinterested as the being which made him: he is profound in his views, and accurate in his judgment *except where knowledge of the world* is necessary to form a judgment. He is so amiable that I pronounce you will love him if ever you become acquainted with him.

Coldly forbidding though many saw him, John Adams had a deeply affectionate, sensuous relationship with his wife, Abigail, his "forever friend," and he marveled at her intellect. Her letters "give me more entertainment than all the speeches I hear," he told her. "There is more good Thoughts, fine strokes and Mother Wit in them than I hear in a whole Week." Gordon Wood has noted that in her correspondence "she quoted from an extraordinary array of writers, often from memory: John Dryden, Alexander Pope, William Collins, Edward Young, Shakespeare, the Bible, Polybius, and Charles Rollin's ancient history, among others." Furthermore, she saw no need to hold her tongue. In 1776, when her husband was engaged in framing new governance, she had written him: "I desire you would remember the ladies and be more generous and favorable to them than your ancestors. Do not put such unlimited power in the hands of husbands. Remember, all men would be tyrants if they could."

At one of their reunions, Adams said to her, "I come to place my head upon your bosom." Imploring her to join him in the capital, he said, "I never wanted you more in my life." Speaking of their farm in Quincy, he told her, "You must come and leave the Place to the mercy of the winds." And, he affirmed, "I can do nothing without you." Years later, as she lay dying, he called her his "dear partner of my life for fifty-four years and for many years more as a lover." Their marriage "constitutes one of the great romances in the history of the American presidency," the biographer John Patrick Diggins has written. "The relationship was a rapture of fused souls." In one letter, she called him "guide, guardian, Husband, lover, friend." After her death, John Adams remembered her as his "best, dearest, worthiest, wisest friend."

With his wife keeping vigil, Adams labored strenuously to make the transition from the George Washington presidency seamless. To legitimate the succession, he ill-advisedly kept on Washington's entire final cabinet, though Washington had appointed Timothy Pickering secretary of state only after six other men had turned down his offer of the post. Furthermore, three of the department heads gave their allegiance not to Adams but to his opponent for control of the Federalist Party, Alexander Hamilton, who, as Ron Chernow has noted, "aspired to be the shadow president." Pickering, in particular, served as Hamilton's spy within the government. (Pickering, Adams jested, would be discontented in Heaven "because he must there . . . acknowledge a superior.") For four years, Adams's Secretary of the Treasury Oliver

Wolcott, when comptroller, had served directly under Hamilton, and Secretary of War James McHenry had performed as best man at Hamilton's wedding. Hamilton, a man of boundless ambition, worked relentlessly to undermine Adams's presidency. "Beware of that spare Cassius," Abigail Adams warned her husband. "O I have read his Heart in his wicked Eyes many a time. The very devil is in them."

Adams had celebrated the American Revolution in 1776 as an event that would be "an Astonishment . . . all over the World in this and in future Generations," and, for decades, he had committed himself to mastering the essentials of constitutionalism so that his prophecy would be fulfilled. "Keep your Law Book or some Point of Law in your mind at least 6 Hours in a day," he had instructed himself. "Study Seneca, Cicero, and all other good moral Writers." Gordon Wood has said of Adams, "No American was more deeply involved in the constitutionalism of the American Revolution. Certainly no one took the Revolution and its significance for politics more seriously, and no one identified his whole life and career with the Revolution and its success more completely." And from his disciplined perusals, he emerged with a conception of the appropriate structure of governance that moved well beyond the Whig disapproval of monarchy he had nurtured in the age of George III.

※·※

A political theorist with a toughminded awareness of fissures in the social fabric, John Adams believed that a strong executive was essential. When, at the constitutional convention, the framers were preoccupied with sorting out the mechanics of federalism, Diggins has maintained, "Adams alone was making the case for the importance of the executive branch." In the massive *A Defence of the Constitutions of Government of the United States of America*, Adams had written, "If there is one certain truth to be collected from the history of all ages, it is this: that the people's rights and liberties, and the democratical mixture in a constitution, can never be preserved without a strong executive."

A president, Adams declared, was "the natural friend of the people, and the only defense which they or their representatives can have against the avarice and ambition [of] great families." Aristocrats were "the most difficult Animals to manage," he later said. (That he was often perceived to be pro-aristocrat, the historian Brian Steele has perceptively written, "only goes to show how effective Adams was at making himself misunderstood.") Adams rebuked Jefferson, "You are afraid of the one—I, of the few. You are apprehensive of Monarchy, I, of Aristocracy." Jefferson, Diggins has commented, "believed that the people would be virtuous if left unmolested by government, while Adams believed that the 'machinery of government' was necessary to make people virtuous." Furthermore, Adams had remarked when revamping the Massachusetts Constitution, that unless the executive was fully empowered, he would be "run down like a Hare before the Hunters."

It should also be acknowledged that, despite his suspicion of the aristocracy, John Adams had a deeply conservative outlook. As a Patriot leader in the age of the Revolution, he deplored "the Spirit of Levelling" and asserted, "There must be a Decency, and Respect, and Veneration introduced for Persons in Authority . . . or We are undone." Proposals to expand the suffrage he thought mischievous. "There will be no End to it," Adams warned. "Women will demand a Vote. Lads from 12 to 21 will think their Rights are not enough attended to, and every Man, who has not a Farthing, will demand an equal Voice . . . in all Acts of State."

Adams sought as president to impose himself between "simplemen" and "gentlemen." He had earlier, under the pseudonym Humphrey Ploughjogger, contended that ordinary folk were "made of as good Clay" as the ostensibly "great ones of the World." Yet he had also come to believe that the masses—whom he once called the "common Herd of Mankind"—had been "as unjust, tyrannical, . . . and cruel as any king or senate." Neither poor nor wealthy "should ever be suffered to be masters," he maintained. "They should have equal power to defend themselves," he had written earlier, and to maintain a proper balance there needed to be an "independent mediator between them, always ready" to aid the weaker.

Yet, as the historian Bruce Miroff has pointed out, "Adams's executive was a curious blend of power and passivity; his hallmark was not energy, but impartiality and integrity. . . . The driving, dominating, committed executive . . . was the opposite of what Adams wanted." Miroff has further maintained, "Serving as the balancing force between social classes, political parties, and legislative branches, the executive might have to move with decisiveness and firmness. Yet, since . . . [Adams] lacked any interest or program of his own, his characteristic stance was to wait." At times, to be sure, Adams did demonstrate a willingness to seize the reins, especially toward the end of his presidency when he asserted himself on foreign policy, but for the most part he took a more limited stance.

With a constrained view of his authority, and denied the backing his party had given unstintingly to his illustrious predecessor, Adams trimmed sails. He saw it as his constitutional duty to present information, and sometimes recommendations, to Congress, but not to influence its deliberations. Not once did he veto a bill. Confronted with a demand for documents generated by negotiations with France, Adams obliged—in keeping with what he had earlier told his wife: "My ideas are very high of the Rights and Powers of the House of Representatives." He also sought to strip the presidency of majestic accoutrements, and he instructed his wife to paint out the family coat of arms that adorned her carriage in Braintree (later called Quincy). The highest-ranked Federalist, Adams eschewed the role of party leader.

Adams diminished the presidency, too, by spending long stretches away in Massachusetts. That did not always matter much. The civil service in 1800 numbered barely three thousand persons, and nine-tenths of them did not work in the capital. When the government moved from Philadelphia to the banks of the Potomac, the accumulated archives of all of the departments over nearly twelve years fit comfortably into seven packing cases. Furthermore, Adams kept in close touch with cabinet officials, especially his secretary of state, when he was away. Still, it was vexing during international crises to have the president of the United States holed up on his farm in Massachusetts, sometimes out of concern for his seriously ill wife, always to savor her affection. In 1799, he dwelt there for eight months. Adams's absences opened him to disparagement. "His stay from the seat of Government . . . is a source of much disgust," one critic said. "It embarrasses the public business and has the air of an abdication."

➤-◄

To an extent he could not have imagined on taking the oath of office, foreign affairs preoccupied Adams and all but devoured his presidency, though they also provided the occasion for his assertion of executive power. "The whole of Adams's single term," the historians Stanley Elkins and Eric McKitrick wrote, "was absorbed, to a degree unequaled in any other American presidency, with a single problem, a crisis in foreign relations." Just two days before Adams took office, France issued a decree imperiling every US ship at sea, and in the summer of 1798 the abrasive conflict with France became a "Quasi-War." Like other Federalists, Adams despised the regimes that emerged from the French Revolution (it was not possible, he said, to create a republic out of twenty million atheists) but, at first, he sought rapprochement. "My Entrance into Office is marked by a Misunderstanding with France, which I shall endeavor to reconcile, provided that no Violation of Faith, no Stain upon Honour, is exacted," he told one of his sons. "America," he asserted, "is not SCARED." Adams, though, was painfully aware that his army numbered fewer than two thousand and his sole naval vessel was an unarmed customs coaster.

When France became even more aggressive, however—capturing US vessels and confiscating valuable cargoes, while snubbing the US envoy—Adams summoned Congress into special session (something that had never been done before) and asked for naval expansion. Congress obliged by authorizing completion of the building of three frigates as well as ships of the line and a dozen smaller ships, and it strengthened coastal fortifications. (One result of this initiative was that the executive branch gained another component: the Navy Department, created in 1798, along with the Marine Corps.) Americans, Adams said, evoking memories of 1776, were not going to display "a colonial spirit of fear and sense of inferiority." In the following year, he rescinded an edict of Washington's that forbade the arming of US merchant vessels. The new frigates and the armed merchantmen soon aroused national pride by routing French warships and privateers.

At times during his presidency, Adams quickened war frenzy, and Congress had to restrain him. He drew cheers when he told one gathering, "The finger of destiny writes on the wall the word War." Though he had never been a soldier, he began appearing in public in full military uniform, sword at his side, on one occasion summoning the youth of Boston: "To arms then, my young friends . . . especially by sea." He refrained, however, from urging a declaration of war. "Great is the Guilt of an unnecessary war," he wrote his wife. Like George Washington, John Adams understood, too, that challenging a European power could result in the extermination of the fragile young republic.

France, though, further provoked Adams by what became known as the XYZ Affair. After he sent three plenipotentiaries to Paris in 1797 to improve Franco-American relations, agents of French Foreign Minister Talleyrand informed the American envoys that no serious negotiations could begin unless they paid that official a bribe of a quarter of a million dollars. ("The French government," the historian Sean Wilentz has asserted, was "marinated in corruption.") Talleyrand also required that the US emissaries agree to lend France $12 million, make other concessions, and induce President Adams to apologize for statements he had made about their country. One official even threatened America with being wiped off the map as the Venetian republic had been. The venal Talleyrand, who had been bullying and mulcting small European states, had convinced himself that the absurdly pretentious republic in the wilderness across the sea "merited no more consideration than Genoa or Geneva," and deserved to be punished for failing to live up to the terms of the alliance with France that had secured its independence. The US commissioners had been ready at the outset to fork over an obligatory douceur, but they were incensed by these excessive demands. And Adams, believing that the United States was "destined beyond a doubt to be the greatest Power on Earth, and that within the Life of Man," would not cower, though he did not welcome a conflict.

Knowing that revelation of this offensive behavior might well stoke an irresistible demand for war, Adams refrained from informing Congress about it, but he was compelled to do so by the Jeffersonian Republican majority, who had only limited knowledge of what had transpired in Paris and were certain that, by failing to release documents, Adams was concealing materials favorable to the French. When, in his role as presiding officer of the Senate, Vice President Jefferson read out the sordid details, with Talleyrand's agents designated X, Y, and Z, his Republican followers were stunned. Abigail Adams, seated in the gallery, reported with delight that "the Jacobins in the Senate & House were struck dumb and opened not their mouths." Jefferson himself acknowledged that the announcement of the dispatches "produced such a shock on the republican mind as has never been seen since our independence." Outraged, the country rallied to Adams, who was identified with a statement attributed to one of the envoys, "Millions for our defense but not one cent for tribute." (The US representative had actually said, "No! No! Not a sixpence!")

To his surprise, Adams found himself a popular figure, cheered as he walked the streets of Philadelphia and hailed by patriots singing a new song, "Adams and Liberty." When a theater company offered "French Songs and Airs," the audience, shouting them down, demanded instead "The President's March." The wife of the British envoy to the United States reported: "The President went to the Play last night for the first time. He is a Presbiterian and goes seldomer into publick than Washington did. . . . Nothing could equal the noise and uproar, the

The sheet music for the *President's March* features an image of John Adams with the caption "Behold the Chief who now commands!" The earlier composition by Philip Phile took on added significance during Adams's conduct of the Quasi-War with France when it was set to the words of "Hail Columbia," a poem by Joseph Hopkinson. A rendition of the song in a Philadelphia theater in 1798, Abigail Adams reported, drew "the most unbounded applause" from the audience, "whilst the thunder from their Hands was incessant." *Library of Congress, LC-M1630.3.H31798 b3*

President's March was played & called for over and over again, it was sung & danced to." But Adams was dismayed by the frenzy of anti-French mobs of rioters who stormed the capital city of Philadelphia.

Though Adams had to cope with war hysteria, he won the hearts of peace-loving Americans by criticizing the efforts of Federalists in Congress to create a provisional army to repel a French invasion. That proposal was strongly supported by Southerners fearful that the French would move from their Caribbean base to invade plantations with the aim of sparking slave insurrections. "There is no more prospect of seeing a French Army here than there is in Heaven," Adams believed, especially after Admiral Nelson's devastating triumph on the Nile. He sought to expand the navy not to fight but to prevent a war. When Congress prevailed, Adams asked George Washington to assume command of the provisional army, but Washington accepted only after saying it was unlikely that he would take the field and insisting on naming his next in command as well as other officers, an unexpected affront to Adams.

Secretary of State Pickering took it on himself to write Washington, "If any considerations should prevent your taking command of the army, I deceive myself extremely if you will not think it should be conferred on Colo. Hamilton," and Alexander Hamilton pressed his ambition for preferment, though other veterans of the Patriot cause of 1776 outranked him. The general's choice of Hamilton as his deputy put that highly partisan Federalist in actual command of the armed forces. Dismayed, Adams later told Washington, who had behaved badly in his role of ex-president, "You crammed him down my throat." (Washington, though, did refuse to support the Federalists when they conspired to sabotage Adams's attempts to maintain peace. In the autumn of 1799, a month before his death, the first president said that "the vessel is afloat or very nearly so. . . . I shall trust to the mariners whose duty it is to watch, to steer it into a safe port.")

President Adams bears a share of the blame for the worst feature of the anti-Jacobin zealotry fostered by the Quasi-War: the Alien and Sedition Acts of 1798. Together with a law lengthening the naturalization period from five to fourteen years, the Alien Acts, one of which empowered the president to deport suspected subversives, were aimed by Federalists at recent arrivals, some of them enthusiasts for the French Revolution who gravitated toward the Republicans. Secretary Pickering wanted to employ the Alien statutes for mass deportations, but Adams refused. Numbers of French émigrés, however, fled the country, one of them muttering, "Everywhere one saw murderous glances." Considerably more troubling was the Sedition Act, which stipulated imprisonment for "uttering or publishing any false, scandalous and malicious writing . . . against the government of the United States, or either house of the Congress . . . with intent to . . . excite against them . . . the hatred of the good people of the United States." Supreme Court justices, riding circuit, traveled from town to town to search out suspect behavior that could expose individuals to prosecution.

Adams did not ask for this legislation, but he did not veto it, and he helped create the atmosphere that fostered it. He lashed out against a "thousand tongues of calumny," perhaps having in mind journalists such as the one who wrote of "the blind, bald, toothless, querulous ADAMS" and called him "a ruffian deserving of the curses of mankind." Incensed at the firebrand Thomas Cooper, the president said that one of this English émigré's articles was a "libel against the whole government and, as such, ought to be prosecuted." Subsequently, Cooper, an esteemed political theorist, was sentenced to six months in prison and fined. True, Adams refused to let Pickering have blank warrants to employ when the president was away or to let him deport the famed British scientist Joseph Priestley, an outspoken secularist who, it was charged, "joining chemic with religion's hate / try'd to decompose church and state." But he did authorize prosecutions and indictments, all of them against Jeffersonians. When Pickering informed him that he regarded an issue of the *Aurora*, a fiercely anti-administration journal, as "imbued with rather more impudence than is common to that paper" and that he was calling on the government's attorney, William Rawle, to prosecute its associate editor, Adams retorted that "if Mr. Rawle does not think the paper libelous, he is not fit for his office; and if he does not prosecute, he will not do his duty."

Adams also rejected appeals for pardons, including a petition by thousands of Vermonters on behalf of their congressman, Matthew Lyon, a combustible Irishman who had spat in the eye of a taunting fellow congressman and who had been re-elected from a jail cell. After his release, Lyon's supporters gave him a long victory lap by transporting him from Vergennes in Vermont's Lake Champlain environs all the way to the US House of Representatives in Philadelphia.

The Alien and Sedition Acts under Adams have gone down in the history books as the first chapter in a notorious succession of violations of civil liberties by American presidents, but certain considerations command our attention. Some of the publications under fire were in truth vicious. "Had any one other than Adams been President at the time, it is probable that the Alien and Sedition Acts would

have been passed anyway," the journalism historian James Pollard has
written. Pollard concluded: "Considering the temper of the times,
relatively few prosecutions were brought under these obnoxious laws
and the resulting convictions were still fewer." Moreover, the provisions of the sedition statute actually liberalized the common law.
Prosecutors were required to prove intent to defame; there was no
prior restraint on publication; and the accused were accorded jury
trials. Adams, it should also be noted, was not the only president to advocate suppression. George Washington favored "laws against aliens . . .
who acknowledge *no allegiance* to this Country, and in many instances
are sent among us . . . for the *express purpose* of poisoning the minds of
our people and to sow dissension among them."

In protest of federal prosecutions, Jefferson secretly drafted resolutions for consideration by the Kentucky legislature denouncing the
Sedition law as an unconstitutional transgression that could drive states
"into revolution and blood." In the companion Virginia Resolutions,
Madison lamented an aggrandizement of executive power that threatened "the transformation of the republican system of the United
States into a monarchy," but put his trust in federal courts. Since the
Constitution was no more than a "compact," Jefferson maintained,
states had the right to reject illegitimate acts as "void, and of no force"
within their borders—a doctrine Jefferson called nullification. The
Kentucky Resolution, the historian James Morton Smith wrote,
"was potentially as dangerous to the Union as the oppressive laws
were to individual liberty." Neither the Kentucky nor the Virginia
Resolutions, however, Brian Steele has maintained, "advocated—or
even broached—secession."

The government encountered a different form of dissent in a local
remonstrance against a direct tax levied to finance the struggle with
France. Once again, it took place in Pennsylvania, but this time in the
"Dutch" (German) communities in the eastern part of the state. It
was led by John Fries, an auctioneer who had been a militia captain in
the war against the redcoats and who, far from being a radical, voted
Federalist. Encouraged by Fries, a mob broke into a Bethlehem jail

and freed imprisoned tax dodgers. Adams responded by dispatching thousands of troops. Though the dissenters offered no armed resistance, Fries and two of his comrades were arrested, convicted, and sentenced to hang. Hamilton and every member of the cabinet strongly favored carrying out the death sentence as a deterrent, asserting that hangings would infuse "the malevolent and fractious with terror." But the president, after scrutinizing the evidence, concluded that the episode constituted a riot, not an act of treason, and spared the lives of the three men—a stroke of mercy that infuriated the Hamilton cadre.

This action indicated that Adams harbored mounting misgivings about the multifold costs and risks of undeclared war with France, fearing that the longer the conflict persisted, the greater was the danger to domestic tranquility from the expanded army. Especially alarming was Hamilton's thirst to lead forces into Virginia to subdue Jeffersonian Republicans in the Old Dominion. Coded messages exposed that Hamilton planned to move south from Virginia at the head of an expanded army to seize Spanish territory on the Gulf Coast, then to invade Mexico. He also said, "We ought to squint at South America," with the expectation that he would return home, a man on horseback, hailed as conquering commander. Hamilton, Jefferson surmised, could be "our Buonaparte." Hamilton also sought to instigate an insurrection in the president's cabinet. "If the Chief is too desultory," he wrote Secretary McHenry, "his Ministers ought to be more united. . . . Break this subject to our friend *Pickering*. His views are sound and energetic; and try together to bring the other Gentlemen to a consultation. If . . . it is wished, send for me & I will come." Adams, however, was steadfast. Though Congress had authorized enlarging the army, he quietly refrained from issuing recruiting orders.

In February 1799, over vocal objections from Hamilton's agents in his cabinet, Adams, consulting no one, announced that he planned to negotiate with the French government. "Of all the brave acts of his career," his biographer David McCullough wrote, Adams's message to the Senate submitting the nomination of a minister plenipotentiary to the French Republic "was perhaps the bravest." For eight months, the president delayed sending his envoy until France gave credible assurances that the American representative would be properly received. The hiatus also provided time for launching more US warships to enhance the envoy's bargaining position. Hamilton urged Adams to cancel the mission, and, in Massachusetts, Federalist leaders erased a passage in the governor's Thanksgiving Proclamation requesting the blessing of God on the peace endeavor. To placate critics, Adams added two members to the delegation but insisted on men of his own pacific disposition, Governor William Davie of North Carolina and Chief Justice Oliver Ellsworth. In sum, John Adams used his role as commander in chief adroitly, not for war but for peace. His performance maddened the Ultra Federalists. Their "rage," Adams said later, "appeared to me then, and has appeared to me ever since, an absolute Delirium." They resolved to sabotage the peace initiative, but Adams outwitted them.

The mission met with success. Less than a week after the Americans arrived in Paris, they were cordially received by both Talleyrand and Napoleon, and on September 30, 1800, the French signed a pact agreeing to US demands. The Convention of Mortefontaine of 1800 liberated the United States from the 1778 treaty of alliance with France, renewed diplomatic relations between the two countries in a spirit of "true and sincere Friendship," restored commercial relations on a most-favored-nation basis, secured the release of American vessels, and, by establishing "a firm, inviolable, and universal peace," ended the vexing Quasi-War. (Ultras, however, had so delayed the dispatch of the mission that news of the end to war came too late to gain Adams credit for his feat in his bid for re-election.) Though peace owed more to the disinclination of Talleyrand and Napoleon to engage in a diversionary conflict with the United States than to American actions, the historian Edward Channing called the president's action "one of the most fortunate bits of negotiation that ever took place." Adams had grounds for his own assessment of the outcome: "a diamond in my crown." His resolve to send a mission to Paris, Adams said, was "the most disinterested, the most determined, and the most successful of my whole life."

As the president intended, the treaty also deflated Alexander Hamilton's dreams of imperial power. "All of Hamilton's hopes for military glory died with Adams's decision," Joseph Ellis has written. "For over a year Hamilton continued to work feverishly on the logistical and organizational details for a phantom army that chiefly existed only in his own imagination." Abigail Adams had the immense satisfaction, as she stood by Hamilton's side, of witnessing the disbanding of the New Army. John Adams later wrote of Hamilton: "Born on a Speck more obscure than Corsica . . . with infinitely less courage and Capacity than Bonaparte, he would in my Opinion, if I had not controlled the fury of his Vanity, . . . involved us in all the Bloodshed and distractions of foreign and civil War at once."

On November 1, 1800, the Quasi-War at last behind him, Adams moved into the President's Mansion, as it was then called, in the Federal City (not yet officially designated Washington, DC). "May none but honest and wise Men ever rule under this roof," Adams prayed, as he asked for "the best of Blessings on this House and all that shall hereafter inhabit it." George Washington had chosen the site for the building, which was designed by the Irish architect James Hoban on the model of the Georgian country house of the Duke of Leinster, and, together with the French architect, Pierre L'Enfant, Washington had laid out a majestic plan for the capital.

But the shabby village where Adams resided sat in mosquito-infested marshes with nothing but protruding tree stumps to relieve a dismal vista of muddy streets and what a cabinet member said were "small miserable huts." A Connecticut congressman called the city "both melancholy and ludicrous." When Americans held fast to the vision of a magnificent city in classical style, renaming Goose Creek the Tiber, Europeans were amused. The Irish poet Thomas Moore later wrote of "this embryo capital, where fancy sees / Squares in morasses, obelisks in trees," and a Continental commentator scoffed: "Voilà un Capitol sans Ciceron; voici le Tibre sans Rome." There was "not a Chair fit to sit in," Adams informed his wife about their new abode: "The Beds and Bedding are in a woeful Pickle. . . . There is not a Carpet, nor a Curtain, nor a Glass [mirror], nor Linnen, nor China, nor any Thing." Damp plaster was still drying on the walls; stairways were missing; there was no firewood; and Abigail Adams became a legendary figure by hanging wash in what later would be the East Room of the White House.

⋇

In the campaign of 1800, Adams, seeking re-election, had the misfortune of confronting formidable opposition in Thomas Jefferson and a Republican Party animated by contempt for the president. Not satisfied with dwelling on legitimate issues such as the Sedition Act, Jefferson's supporters falsely accused Adams of being a covert monarchist who had schemed to marry one of his sons to a daughter of George III until Washington, allegedly drawing a sword with the intent of running Adams through, forced him to back down. Adams's foes also charged that he had dispatched C. C. Pinckney to Europe to fetch four mistresses, two for the envoy and two for the president. (If so, Adams retorted, "Pinckney had kept them all for himself and cheated me out of my two.")

The notorious scribbler whom Jefferson hired to defame Adams, one James Callender, called the president a "wretch," a "repulsive pedant," "one of the most egregious fools upon the continent," and a "hideous hermaphroditical character, which has neither the force and firmness of a man, nor the gentleness and sensibility of a woman." Jefferson denied that he ever employed Callender and persuaded himself of this false claim, leading Joseph Ellis to conclude that for the devious man "the deepest secrets were not the ones he kept from his enemies but the ones he kept from himself." (Two years later, after a falling out, Callender turned on Jefferson by writing, "It is well known that the man . . . keeps, and for many years past has kept, as his concubine, one of his own slaves. Her name is SALLY. . . . By this wench Sally, our President has had several children. There is not an individual in the neighbourhood of Charlottesville who does not believe the story, and not a few who know it." In the late twentieth century, biographers acknowledged, some of them reluctantly, that Jefferson had indeed impregnated his young slave Sally Hemings and had kept their offspring in bondage.)

Republicans drummed especially on Jefferson's charge that Adams, bewitched by the "glare of royalty" in the "harlot" England, championed the monarchy. One critic found it incredible "that every measure and every pretense of the stupid and selfish Stuarts should be adopted by the posterity of those who fled from their madness and tyranny to the distant and dangerous wilds of America." The disposition of "Royalist" Adams toward monarchy, foes alleged, could be detected in the writings of the so-called Duke of Braintree. Years later, Adams wrote Jefferson: "I will forfeit my life if you can find one sentence in Defence of the Constitutions or the Discourses on Davila which, by a fair construction, can favour the introduction of Monarchy or Aristocracy to America. They were all written to Support and Strengthen the Constitution of the United States." On another occasion, he told Jefferson, "If you suppose that I have ever had a design or desire of attempting to introduce . . . a hereditary Executive, . . . you are wholly mistaken." Adams, though, may have protested a bit too much. He had, at least in conversation, been reported as saying that "no people could be happy without an hereditary first magistrate."

Adams had to cope with opposition not only from Republicans but also from Ultras. Within his own ranks, Secretary of State Pickering, who regarded the president as a dodderer "influenced by the vilest passions," and other Hamilton vassals sabotaged his bid for re-election. Much too belatedly, Adams fired Pickering, who was leaking official documents to Hamilton and had been impeding the president's efforts to end the Quasi-War. Adams first gave Pickering an opportunity to resign, but the cabinet minister said that, given his debts and the burden of a large family, he needed the salary of his office. The president promptly replied that on account of "diverse causes & considerations" affecting the government, "you are hereby discharged." (Adams then named John Marshall to the post, and Marshall proved to be a thoroughly reliable secretary of state.) The president also forced Secretary of War James McHenry to step down. Like Pickering, McHenry was both perfidious and incompetent.

Hamilton, who conspired to deny Adams another term by sneaking electoral votes away to the Federalist vice-presidential nominee, unleashed a vitriolic fifty-four-page pamphlet assailing Adams for permitting his "disgusting egotism" to "deprive him of self-command and produce very outrageous behavior." Beset by "a vanity without bounds," Adams had "a jealousy capable of discoloring every subject." The president, Hamilton wanted the nation to know, "does not possess the talents adapted to the Administration of Government, and . . . there are great and intrinsic defects in his character, which unfit him for the office of Chief Magistrate." When McHenry sent a report on his final session with Adams, in which the president had accused Hamilton of scheming, Hamilton retorted that Adams "is more mad than I ever thought him and, I shall soon be led to say, as wicked as he is mad." (Adams, in turn, so despised Hamilton that he called him the "bastard brat of a Scotch Pedlar," and charged that Hamilton was known for his "fornications, adulteries, and his incests." In 1807, Adams said of Hamilton that "like the Worm at the Root of the Peach, did he labor for twelve years, underground and in darkness, to girdle the Root.")

Alexander Hamilton's invective injured him more than Adams. Even an Arch Federalist, reporting sentiment in Massachusetts, wrote, "Our friends lamented the publication. . . . Not a man . . . but condemns it." The New England Federalist Noah Webster thought the pamphlet "little short of insanity." Moreover, while preparing his screed, which Ron Chernow has called "a crazily botched job, an extended tantrum in print," Hamilton wrote Adams demanding satisfaction for his "base, wicked, and cruel calumny," language implying that he was challenging the president of the United States to a duel. (Alexander Hamilton's reputation had earlier suffered a blow when, in response to the accusation that he had diverted public funds to a speculator, the former treasury secretary acknowledged that he had given the man money but only as blackmail after carrying on a sexual relationship with the man's wife. "My crime," he insisted, "is an amorous connection." Hamilton's wife first learned of this "connection" when she was in labor with their sixth child.)

In addition to other difficulties he had to surmount in 1800, Adams sustained damage for one particular action whose wide reverberations among American voters he could not anticipate. In response to a British demand, he surrendered to them a sailor who had been a ringleader of what has been called "the bloodiest mutiny in British naval history." The sailor then claimed to be an American. He was lying, but the president's critics who took up the sailor's claim made it appear that the president, abandoning America's commitment to freedom, was collaborating in impressment. Federalist campaigners pronounced Adams guilty of the murder of this "martyr to liberty."

Those Federalists who, unlike Hamilton, remained loyal to Adams outdid Republicans in the ferocity of their attacks on the president's rival in the 1800 campaign. When they were not informing voters that Thomas Jefferson was readying a guillotine, they were calling him an "intellectual voluptuary." A Connecticut editor foresaw that in a Jefferson presidency "murder, robbery, rape, adultery, and incest will be openly taught and practiced," while another ardent Federalist asked, "Can serious and reflecting men . . . doubt that, if Jefferson is elected, and the Jacobins get into authority, . . . those morals which protect our lives from the knife of the assassin—which guard the chastity of our wives and daughters from seduction and violence—defend our property from plunder and devastation, and shield our religion from contempt and profanation, will not be trampled upon and exploded?" The president of Yale University echoed these sentiments. "If Jefferson is elected," Timothy Dwight affirmed, "the Bible would be cast into a bonfire, our holy worship changed into a dance of Jacobin Phrensy, our wives and daughters dishonored, and our sons converted into the disciples of Voltaire and the dragoons of Marat." Still, these men found it hard to believe that the Lord would "permit a howling atheist to sit at the head of this nation."

Since electors were chosen by legislators in more than two-thirds of the states, with no set calendar, the 1800 contest required nearly a year to be resolved, and the balloting had a scary sequel. When the Republican caucus in Congress nominated Thomas Jefferson and the New Yorker Aaron Burr, it fully intended that Jefferson would become president and Burr vice president. But so strong had party discipline become such a short time after parties were founded that Jefferson and Burr got identical electoral totals, and, since no candidate had a majority, the election was thrown into the House of Representatives, with each state, irrespective of the size of its delegation, having one vote. Despite the intent of the caucus, the wily Burr, grandson of the legendary theologian Jonathan Edwards but with little of the divine in his outlook, did not make clear that he would count himself out, and the Federalists, though the Adams ticket had been defeated, fished in muddied waters. Moreover, the outcome would be determined by the Federalist-controlled Congress, many of whose members were lame ducks who had just been rejected. On the first ballot, conducted in the melodramatic setting of a fierce blizzard besieging the capital, Jefferson, who needed nine of the sixteen states for a majority, carried eight, Burr six, with two uncommitted. Over a wrenching stretch of time, that deadlock continued.

After thirty-five ballots with no resolution in sight, a crisis loomed. President Adams brooded that civil war was imminent, and Jefferson said that many of his Republican supporters were contemplating resort to force to prevent the frustration of the popular will. The divide, Jefferson said, "opens upon us an abyss, at which every sincere patriot must shudder." Republicans feared that Federalist conspirators might carry out a coup that would put Burr in power or, more likely, that Congress would let Adams's term expire and leave the country without a president for nearly a year. When Congress reconvened in December, it might choose a Federalist for president. To avert either possibility, the Republican governor of Pennsylvania mustered the state militia and implied recourse to artillery. Later, the prominent Jeffersonian Albert Gallatin reported, "If any man should be thus appointed President . . . and accept the office, he would instantaneously be put to death."

Then, altogether unexpectedly, an improbable figure came to Jefferson's side. Alexander Hamilton, though saying of Jefferson "his politics are tinctured with fanaticism; . . . he is too much in earnest with his democracy; . . . he has been a mischievous enemy to the principal measures of our past administration," still thought him preferable to Burr, a schemer "without Scruple" who would "listen to no monitor but his ambitions." Hamilton wrote a cabinet official: "As to *Burr*, there is nothing in his favor. His private character is not defended by his most partial friends. . . . He is truly the *Catiline* of America." Jefferson, Hamilton declared, "is by far not so dangerous a man and he has pretensions to character." Moreover, there was "no fair reason to suppose him capable of being corrupted." Perhaps because of Hamilton's influence, perhaps because of anxiety about civil strife, perhaps because Jefferson struck a deal in which he agreed to preserve some Federalist influence (though he had vowed not to do so), perhaps because of some combination of these, Jefferson prevailed. The Senate then went on to elect Burr vice president.

No one wanted the country to go through such an ordeal again, and, as a consequence, Congress adopted the Twelfth Amendment to the Constitution, providing that henceforth electors would make distinct choices, one for president, one for vice president. In September 1804, enough states ratified it. That remedy, by altering the plan of the Framers, safeguarded the nation from the possibility of another perilous stalemate—but at a cost. In devising what turned out to be a troublesome scheme, the Framers had anticipated that electors would choose the two best men in America, so that if the president died or was incapacitated, someone of similarly high quality would take over. Once the two offices were separated, however, party leaders did not always give serious thought to vetting running mates, and, too often, obscure and clueless "Throttlebottoms" were chosen, though they were "only a heartbeat away" from the presidency.

Jefferson later called his triumph "the revolution of 1800," which, he claimed, was "as real a revolution in the principles of our government as that of '76 was in its form; not affected . . . by the sword, as that, but by the rational and peaceable instrument of reform, the suffrage of the people." (He believed, Joseph Ellis has explained, that his victory signified "a renewal of the principles of '76.") Cued by Jefferson, history texts present the 1800 election as a milestone in the march of democracy. Yet Jefferson had only an eight-vote edge over Adams in the Electoral College, and he won because the Constitution magnified the political leverage of the South by counting three-fifths of its slaves in allotting electoral votes. Of Jefferson's electoral total of seventy-three, all but twenty came from below the Potomac. If Jefferson's total had not been inflated by the three-fifths provision, Adams would have gained a second term. As a sardonic New England editor wrote, Jefferson rode "into the TEMPLE OF LIBERTY upon the *shoulders of slaves.*" Furthermore, save for the state of New York where Burr mounted an effective campaign for the Republicans, Adams ran better than he had four years earlier, and he outperformed the Federalist slate for Congress.

Still, if the outcome did not constitute a revolution, it was highly significant, for it marked the end of the Federalist era. Adams could not survive resentment at the high taxes required to support the bloated military establishment; in 1799, the Adams government spent twice as much as the George Washington administration had toward the end of its tenure. There was even a stamp tax that evoked unwelcome memories of Patriot anger at the Crown in the eighteenth century. The election of 1800 signaled, too, the resumption of reign by the Virginia Dynasty. Starting with George Washington, and interrupted only by the single term of John Adams, Virginians would control the presidency for thirty-two of the republic's first thirty-six years.

John Patrick Diggins has underscored an even more important feature of the contest. "Instead of a revolution," he writes, "the election of 1800 marked the first time that a government, deriving from a violent revolution, went on to enjoy a peaceful and orderly transfer of power [from one party to another]. The outs had replaced the ins, and not a shot was fired nor a back stabbed, no guillotines and no knifing in the bathtub of Jean-Paul Marat by Charlotte Corday, symbolizing a liberty born of reason killed by enthusiasm."

＊＊

The troubled presidency of John Adams ended in profound sadness. "My little bark has been oversett in a Squall of Thunder & Lightning and hail attended with a Strong Smell of Sulphur," he wrote his youngest son. On the very day that electors rejected him, the president learned that his son Charles, aged thirty, had died of cirrhosis of the liver—the consequence of addiction to alcohol. "The melancholy decease of your Brother is an Affliction of a more serious nature to this Family than any other. Oh! that I had died for him if that would have relieved him from his faults as well as his disease." (His words were no doubt heartfelt, but they may also have derived from guilt, for he had earlier said of Charles, "I renounce him," adding, "King David's Absalom had some ambition and some Enterprize. Mine is a mere Rake, Buck, Blood, and Beast.")

Bereft but indefatigable, Adams soldiered on with undiminished energy. "I am not about to write Lamentations or Jeremiads over my fate nor Panegyricks upon my life and Conduct," he averred. An outbreak of fire at the neighboring Treasury building did not find him wanting. One newspaper reported: "Through the exertions of the citizens, animated by the example of the President of the United States (who on this occasion fell into the ranks and aided in passing the buckets), the fire was at length subdued." Undismayed by his defeat in the 1800 election, Adams regarded it as a testament to his virtue. "It meant," Joseph Ellis has written, "that political motives had played no role in shaping his policies, which had only the long-term interests of the American republic as a guide." Ellis further maintains that "what died" with the 1800 defeat "was the presumption, so central to Adams's sense of politics and of himself, that there was a long-term collective interest for the republic that was divorced from partisanship," in contrast to Jefferson's recognition that "the American president must forever . . . be the head of a political party."

Adams took advantage of the little time remaining in his term to overhaul the third branch of the federal government. The Judiciary Act of 1801 doubled the number of circuit courts. No longer would US Supreme Court justices be compelled to ride circuit, an arduous requirement that made it difficult to recruit prominent attorneys for the highest tribunal. The Federalist statute also had partisan aspects, for it reduced the size of the Supreme Court as well, denying Jefferson the opportunity to reconfigure the Court through filling vacancies. Federalists, Republicans alleged, had raced to choose last-minute appointees for the twenty-three new slots in lower tribunals created by the law, men derided as "midnight judges." (In fact, the appointments had been made not at midnight but weeks earlier, though after it was known that there would be a change of parties.) Adams and the Federalists, a Republican congressman charged, had reduced the courts to "an hospital for decayed politicians." Still, the Judiciary Act of 1801 was a significant contribution to erecting the structure of the national government set forth in 1787. Adams had an even greater impact on the history of the young republic by naming as Chief Justice of the United States his secretary of state, John Marshall. Over the next third of a century, the Marshall Court legitimated national power and safeguarded property rights.

The third branch also passed judgment on one of President Adams's actions, for the Quasi-War provided the first occasion since the constitutional convention to examine the metes and bounds of a president's authority. In *Little v. Bareme* (1804), handed down after Adams left office, the US Supreme Court ruled that when he ordered US commanders to seize ships sailing to and from French ports, he was violating an act of Congress authorizing interdiction only of vessels headed *toward* French ports. (An American captain named Little had seized a French frigate that had just weighed anchor in a French West Indian port, and the owner of the vessel had brought suit.) Though he is commander in chief, a president may not issue instructions to military and naval officers inconsistent with policies Congress has established by statute, the Court declared.

On March 4, 1801, the day that Jefferson was to be inaugurated, Adams stepped aboard the morning stage at 4:00 AM and rode north toward Massachusetts in the dark. Critics at the time and historians subsequently have accused the president of ill grace in fleeing town on his rival's big occasion. But in a republic only beginning to create traditions, it had not yet been established that departing presidents should take part in a successor's festivities, and Adams left at such an early hour because, if he failed to do so, he could not get as far as Baltimore that day. Especially after his son's death, he had good reason to hasten to Quincy to comfort, and be comforted by, his beloved wife.

However understandable his early leave-taking, the president who was exiting the capital was in truth a man of woe. He blamed his "banishment" not only on the hostility of the Jeffersonians but also on members of his own party, saying "I had nothing but insolence and scurillity from the federalists." In summing up the reason for his downfall, he said, "Jefferson had a party, Hamilton had a party, but the commonwealth had none." To convey his feelings about what Joyce Appleby has called his "vexed presidency," Adams wrote: "I have compared myself to an animal I have seen take hold of the end of a cord with his teeth and be drawn slowly up by pullies through a storm of squibs, crackers, and rockets, flaming and blazing round him every moment; and though the scorching flames made him groan and moan and roar, he would not let go his hold till he had reached the ceiling of a lofty theatre, where he hung some time . . . and at last descended through another storm of burning powder."

Adams also had some intimation of how he would be remembered. Accounts of the period, he said, would state "that Dr Franklins electrical Rod Smote the Earth and out Sprung General Washington. That Franklin electrified him with his Rod—and thence forward these two conducted all the Policy Negotiations Legislation and War." Gordon Wood has advanced a more serious consideration. "Jefferson,"

Wood has written, "told the American people what they wanted to hear—how exceptional they were. Adams told them what they needed to know—truths about themselves that were difficult to bear. Over the centuries Americans have tended to avoid Adams's message; they have much preferred to hear Jefferson's praise of their uniqueness." Scholars have reflected both that attitude and Adams's foreboding. Thomas Bailey has contended that Adams was "temperamentally un-fitted to be President" and "in some respects . . . was a flat failure," while Fred Greenstein has concluded that "Adams' one-term presi-dency suffered from a political ineptness that seemed almost willful." In another assessment, Bruce Miroff has charged Adams with being "premodern, lacking a sense both of executive initiative and of ex-ecutive partisanship."

To be sure, Adams tried to make the best of his lot. "Griefs upon Griefs! Disappointments upon Disappointments," he once wrote a friend. "What then? This is a gay, merry World notwithstanding." But after decades in the public realm, he found it hard to imagine a future for himself. "Something I must do," he said, "or ennui will rain upon me in buckets." Furthermore, he knew how many in Washington, numbers of them in his own disintegrating Federalist Party, were glad that he would no longer be around. Still, he anticipated that, though ennui could be "worse than one of our north-east storms; . . . the la-bors of agriculture and amusement of letters will shelter me." Years later, however, he remarked, "No man who ever held the office of President would congratulate a friend on obtaining it."

⊶⊷

Still, Adams could look back on his four years as chief executive with considerable pride. "After the 3rd of March I am to be a private citizen," Adams remarked. "I shall leave the State with the Coffers full and the fair prospect of a Peace with all the World smiling in its face, its commerce flourishing, its Navy glorious, its agriculture un-commonly productive. . . . O, my Country! May peace be within thy walls, and prosperity within thy palaces." Even the embittered Arch

Federalist Theodore Sedgwick acknowledged, "The President, under circumstances the most trying and discouraging, has acted . . . a noble part. . . . Regardless of the attacks that have been made on his character, he has exhibited a manly fortitude & a dignified composure."

Scholars viewing the span of his career have been especially impressed by his intellectual range. The British historian Esmond Wright has concluded that "as a political thinker Adams was perhaps the most original and, with Madison, the best read in constitutional history and law of all the Founders," a judgment echoing that of the renowned theologian Theodore Parker who in the transcendentalism era declared that "with the exception of Dr. Franklin . . . no American politician of the eighteenth century was Adams's intellectual superior." In 1780, Adams explained his concentration by saying, "I must study Politicks and War that my sons may have the liberty to study Mathmaticks and Philosophy. My sons ought to study Geography, natural History, Naval Architecture, navigation, Commerce and Agriculture, in order to give their Children a right to study Painting, Poetry, Musick, Architecture, Statuary, Tapestry, and Porcelaine."

Dispassionate scholars have expressed admiration, too, for how Adams sculpted the office of chief executive adumbrated by the founders. Leonard White has stated that "Adams confirmed the character of the presidency as the Constitutional Convention had outlined it and as Washington had already formed it." Diggins credits Adams with "prescient modernism" in recognizing that "the growth of the state was not a menace to democracy but would make possible the expansion of popular rights." In *On Revolution*, Hannah Arendt, the sensitive analyst of the horrors of the Holocaust, has celebrated Adams as one of the few statesmen of his time to recognize that for a revolution such as that of 1776 to be significant it required an institutional sequel.

Diggins observes, "though he can scarcely be called an event-making president . . . , those who knew Adams, including some of his enemies, felt themselves in the presence of a rare and virtuous character." At the outset of his term, Adams had told Washington, "It will be happy . . . if it is honorable." And certainly it had been that.

"I pray Heaven to bestow the best of Blessings on this House and all that shall hereafter inhabit it. May none but honest and wise Men ever rule under this roof." These words appeared in a letter that John Adams wrote in 1800 to his wife Abigail, the first occupants of what would become known as the White House. President Adams's plea was carved into the mantel of the State Dining Room in 1945 during the administration of Franklin D. Roosevelt. *White House Collection/White House Historical Association*

The tenure of John Adams taught historians that in assessing a president they should focus not just on policies but on character. David McCullough, however, lamented: "Popular symbolism has not been very generous toward Adams. There is no memorial, no statue . . . in his honor in our nation's capital and to me that is absolutely inexcusable. It's long past time when we should recognize what he did and who he was."

Commenting on the accession of the second American president, the historian Charles Akers observed, "The true test of the Constitution was at hand: Could the office be transferred by the first contested presidential election to another from whom there emanated no aura of superhuman greatness?" A Spanish envoy, noting that only Washington's exalted status had spared the country "internal dissention," anticipated that without the first president, "disunion" would ensue. No successor could hope to equal George Washington's hold on the affections of the American people or his achievements in launching the new government, but John Adams had shown a quiet competence and had even won some popular favor, at least during the patriotic ardor following the XYZ Affair. He had no doubt of what History would say his greatest accomplishment had been. He was to write, "I desire No other Inscription over my Grave Stone than:'Here lies John Adams, who took upon himself the Responsibility of the Peace with France in the Year 1800.'"

4

Thomas Jefferson

Limiting the Government While Creating an Empire

After the nasty campaign and the unnerving melodrama of the presidential balloting in the House of Representatives, the blissful inauguration ceremony on March 4, 1801, seemed especially felicitous. Those who observed Chief Justice John Marshall administer the oath to Thomas Jefferson fully comprehended the significance of the event. The rulers of the country were turning over the reins of power to their opponents in a transfer carried out amicably, even routinely. The thought of not surrendering his authority or of a coup d'état had not crossed Adams's mind. The wife of the editor of the federal city's leading newspaper, the *National Intelligencer*, described Jefferson's inauguration as "one of the most interesting scenes a free people can ever witness. The changes of administration, which in every government and in every age have most generally been epochs of confusion, villainy and bloodshed, in this our happy country take place without any species of distraction, or disorder."

Jefferson, a poor speaker with a thin voice, had a hard time making himself heard that day, which was unfortunate, for his beautifully crafted inaugural address is among the most cherished in the annals of American governance. He began by enunciating his Republican conviction that "the will of the majority is in all cases to prevail," a sentiment far removed from those of most of the Framers. But he stressed

This portrait by Charles Willson Peale captures the dashing and patrician figure of the third president of the new republic. Before his election to the highest office in the land, Jefferson had crafted the Declaration of Independence. The youthful face in this painting suggests the Jefferson of that triumphant earlier period more than the experience of his troubled presidency. *Independence National Historical Park Collection*

that "this sacred principle, . . . to be rightful, must be reasonable; that the minority possess their equal rights, which equal laws must protect, and to violate would be oppression."

Acknowledging the "animation" of the recent campaign, he urged: "Let us restore to social intercourse that harmony and affection without which liberty, and even life itself, are but dreary things. And let us reflect that having banished from our land that religious intolerance under which mankind so long bled and suffered, we have yet gained little if we countenance a political intolerance as despotic, as wicked, and capable of as bitter and bloody persecutions." No doubt bearing some of his Ultra-Federalist critics in mind, he said, "If there be any among us who would wish to dissolve this Union or to change its republican form, let them stand undisturbed as monuments of the safety with which error of opinion may be tolerated where reason is left free to combat it." Aware of the fragility of the constitutional fabric in these first years, Jefferson added:

> I know . . . that some honest men fear that a republican government can not be strong; that this Government is not strong enough. But would the honest patriot, in the full tide of successful experiment, abandon a government which has so far kept us free and firm, on the theoretic and visionary fear that this Government, the world's best hope, may, by possibility, want energy to preserve itself? I trust not. I believe this, on the contrary, the strongest Government on earth. I believe it is the only one where every man, at the call of the law, would fly to the standard of the law, and would meet invasions of the public order as his own personal concern. Sometimes it is said that man cannot be trusted with the government of himself. Can he then be trusted with the government of others? Or have we found angels, in the forms of kings, to govern him? Let history answer this question.

Without alluding to the Sedition Act, the third president celebrated "the diffusion of information, and arraignment of all abuses at the bar of the public reason; freedom of religion; freedom of the press, and freedom of person, under the protection of the Habeas Corpus, and trial by juries impartially selected." Jefferson affirmed: "These principles form the bright constellation which has gone before us and guided our steps through an age of revolution and reformation. . . . They should be the creed of our political faith." Looking back toward the Framers and the heroes of '76, he said that these liberties derived from the "wisdom of our sages and the blood of our heroes." President Jefferson, Joyce Appleby has written, "now moved into the last act of the American Revolution, the one that would disclose the character of the society brought into being in 1776." Jefferson, agreed his friendly biographer Dumas Malone, "embodied the 'spirit of 1776' as fully as any civilian could."

During his presidency, Jefferson also found occasion to enunciate his conviction that governments should not hamper freedom of worship. In Virginia he had fought to disestablish the Anglican Church and to provide space for "the Jew and the Gentile, the Christian and the Mohametan, the Hindoo, and the infidel of every denomination." To Danbury (Connecticut) Baptists during his presidency, he wrote: "Believing with you that religion is a matter which lies solely between Man & his God, that he owes account to none other for his faith or his worship, that the legitimate powers of government reach actions only, & not opinions, I contemplate with sovereign reverence . . . building a wall of separation between Church & State."

⤞⤝

Jefferson swiftly carried these principles into practice by undoing the seamiest transactions of the Adams presidency. He pardoned all ten men, mostly Republican publishers, who had been convicted under the Sedition Act, and got Congress to remit the fines imposed on them, with interest. At his behest, Congress lowered the waiting period for naturalization to five years, where it had been before the Federalists raised it. "Shall oppressed humanity find no asylum on this globe?" he asked. Appalled by defamatory material in Federalist organs, Jefferson nonetheless championed freedom of the press. "I would wish much to see the experiment tried of getting along without public prosecutions for *libels*," he told his attorney general. "I believe we can do it. Patience and well doing, instead of punishment, if it can be found sufficiently efficacious, would be a happy change in the instruments of government." On one occasion, the famed German explorer Alexander von Humboldt came upon a vicious newspaper in the president's office and asked, "Why are these libels allowed?" Jefferson retorted, "Put that paper in your pocket, Baron, and should you hear the reality of our liberty, our freedom of our press, questioned, show this paper, and tell where you found it."

His attitude, his deeds, and the eloquent passages in the inaugural address have won for Jefferson a large reputation as a civil libertarian, but, unhappily, as the historian Leonard Levy has shown, there was a "darker side" to his record. In response to an 1803 inquiry from the governor of Pennsylvania about newspaper criticism of the president and his administration, Jefferson replied, "I have . . . long thought that a few prosecutions of the most prominent offenders would have a wholesome effect in restoring the integrity of the presses," and he furnished an example of how that might be done. Before his presidency ended, his record would be considerably darker.

The Sedition Act also provided Jefferson an opportunity to join issue with the Federalist judiciary, a conflict whose many pitched battles carried on for years. He fired the first shot by proclaiming the law an unconstitutional "nullity." Since the Sedition Act had expired at the end of the Adams presidency, the matter was moot, but he issued the statement defiantly in order to assert that he had as much right as the US Supreme Court to rule on the constitutionality of a statute, for the three branches were co-equals. The Federalists, Jefferson warned, had "retired into the Judiciary as a stronghold . . . and from that battery all the works of republicanism are to be beaten down & erased."

The Jeffersonians especially resented one particular creation of the Federalists: the Judiciary Act of 1801, adopted in the waning weeks of the Adams presidency. It had some sensible features, but Adams had administered it in a flagrantly partisan manner by filling every office with his followers. Jefferson sent a bulletin to numbers of "midnight" officials telling each to regard "the appointment you have received as if never made."

Jefferson's refusal to honor Adams's last appointments led to what has come to be regarded as a landmark Supreme Court decision. When Secretary of State James Madison declined to deliver a commission to William Marbury, a "midnight" appointee as a justice of the peace, Marbury sued for a writ of mandamus. In *Marbury v. Madison*, the US Supreme Court, in an 1803 opinion by John Marshall, scolded the Jefferson administration for denying Marbury and others their rights, but ruled that the section of the Judiciary Act empowering the Court to issue writs of mandamus was unconstitutional. Consequently, Marbury's plea failed. The president took no comfort in this Solomonic decision. True, his administration had escaped unscathed. But Marshall had gone out of his way to berate him. In addition, many accounts contend, the Court established the principle of judicial review—that the Constitution empowers the Supreme Court to invalidate acts of Congress—a doctrine that foretold trouble for presidents and their legislative programs in the future, though not much was made of it at the time. "The judiciary of the United States is the subtle corps of sappers and miners constantly working under ground to undermine the foundations of our confederated fabric," Jefferson protested. "An opinion is huddled up in a conclave, perhaps by a majority of one, delivered as if unanimous, and with the silent acquiescence of lazy or timid associates, by a crafty judge [Marshall] who sophisticates the law to his mind."

Early in the term, Jefferson put through the Judiciary Act of 1802, which eliminated the circuit judgeships launched under Adams, and he and his party also targeted particular Federalist judges. In February 1803, Jefferson called the attention of the House to Judge John Pickering of New Hampshire, who was mentally unbalanced, alcoholic, and incompetent. The House impeached him and the Senate convicted him, removing him from office.

Jefferson also altered the style of the national government by replacing the rococo excess of the Federalists with Doric simplicity. The first president inaugurated in Washington, DC, he appeared at the event without a ceremonial sword. He sold Adams's silver-harnessed presidential coach, and, instead of riding to the inauguration in an elaborate carriage, walked to the capitol. He refused to permit public celebrations of his birthday; discouraged bowing to the president and substituted handshakes; and ended the levees instituted by Washington. Foregoing an appearance before Congress in person at the start of each session, he dispatched written messages because he thought that the behavior of his predecessors smacked of the king's opening address to Parliament.

In addition, to the dismay of foreign diplomats, Jefferson dispensed with internationally recognized rules of etiquette. At weekly dinners, guests were seated without regard to rank. "When brought together in society, all are perfectly equal, whether foreign or domestic, titled or untitled, in or out of office," he insisted. One diplomat, the British minister Anthony Merry, upon arriving in full regalia—plumed hat, coat featuring black velvet and gold braid, dress sword—to present his credentials, was shocked to find the president of the United States of America "not merely in undress, but *actually standing in slippers down at the heels* . . . in a state of negligence actually studied." Americans, however, approved. A congressman who congratulated Jefferson on getting rid of "all the pomp and pageantry which once dishonored our republican institutions" expressed relief that the nation would no longer see a president "drawn to the Capitol by six horses, and . . . gaped at by a wondering multitude."

>-<

In contrast to Hamilton's urban outlook, Jefferson continued to express allegiance to an agrarian idyll. "I think our governments will remain virtuous for many centuries as long as they are chiefly agricultural," he declared. "Those who labour in the earth are the chosen people of God, if ever he had a chosen people." The republic, he maintained, would have the soundest foundation if it rested on families who lived on their own plots of land where they tilled the soil. "While we have land to labor then," Jefferson declared, "let us never wish to see our citizens occupied at a work-bench or twirling a dis-taff.... The mobs of great cities add just so much to the support of pure government as sores do to the strength of the human body."

At Monticello, his hillside estate in Charlottesville, Jefferson indulged these sentiments by creating a rural paradise, though it was one culti-vated not by yeomen farmers but by more than two hundred slaves. In addition to raising a wide range of vegetables, he ordered the planting of well over a thousand peach trees that accompanied cherry, apple, plum, and almond in his orchards, along with vineyards that yielded grapes for wine. The fruit trees gave pleasure by bursting into blossom in springtime. He made careful note, too, of the emergence of the first hyacinths, jonquils, and other flowers, including a Crimson Dark rose.

Jefferson took pride in being a naturalist, one of his many intel-lectual pursuits. He always wanted to be close to nature. Both in Monticello and at the President's House, a pet mockingbird flew about him as he worked. Repeatedly involved in self-generated ex-periments, Jefferson built a collection of specimens including the jaw-bone of a woolly mammoth that he acquired in Kentucky. He also mastered disciplines such as architecture and city planning. He mod-eled his mansion in Virginia on the style of the great Italian archi-tect Palladio, and he transformed the nation's capital by ordering the creation of Pennsylvania Avenue as a lengthy thoroughfare bordered by Lombardy poplars. "Jefferson had the most spacious and encyclo-pedic mind of any of his fellow Americans, including even Benjamin Franklin," Gordon Wood has concluded. "He was interested in more things and knew more about more things than any other American." Jefferson's accomplishments won him high regard abroad and at home. The Marquis de Chastellux characterized Jefferson as "an American who ... is at once a Musician, Drafts man, Geometrician, Astronomer, Natural philosopher, Jurist, and Statesman."

⊰⊱

Jefferson pleased his followers by honoring his campaign pledge of frugality and espousing a circumscribed national state. "The sum of

View of Monticello and Garden, an 1825 watercolor by Jane Braddick Peticolas, depicts Thomas Jefferson's grandchildren in the garden on the west side of Monticello. Jefferson drew inspiration for his hilltop home from the work of the brilliant Italian architect, Palladio. The foreground of the scene calls attention to the Virginia garden that was central to the president's conception of an agrarian republic, though it was maintained by slaves. The many features of the estate included a vineyard whose grapes enabled Jefferson to supplement imports from Europe in his outstanding wine cellar. *Ellen Wayles Randolph Coolidge; by descent to Catherine Coolidge Lastavica; by gift to Thomas Jefferson Foundation, 1986. ©Thomas Jefferson Foundation at Monticello*

good government," he announced in his inaugural address, was leaving men "free to regulate their own pursuits" and not taking "from the mouth of labor the bread it has earned." He maintained that economic pursuits were "most thriving when left most free to individual enterprise." Jefferson declared, "If we can but prevent the government from wasting the labours of the people, under the pretence of taking care of them, they must become happy." Borrowing from the Athenian sage Solon, he expressed his conviction that "no more good must be attempted than the nation can bear."

Unlike Hamilton, who saw the national debt as a way of attracting creditors to the government, Jefferson regarded it as a source of corruption and a burden on taxpayers because servicing the debt incurred by the Federalists devoured almost half of the annual federal revenue. Hence, he embraced the plan of his skillful secretary of the treasury, Swiss-born Albert Gallatin, to retire the debt as quickly as possible by curtailing government functions. In addition, the president persuaded Congress to abolish all internal taxes, including the notorious excise on whiskey that had triggered the rebellion. In the course of his presidency, Jefferson extinguished so many millions of the funded debt that he freed the Treasury of the obligation to pay two million dollars annually in interest. Before long, Jefferson, noting that the government was supported by tariff revenue on imported luxuries purchased by the well-to-do, could ask proudly, "What farmer, what mechanic, what labourer, ever sees a tax-gatherer of the US?"

Jefferson sought to dismantle as much as he could of the executive branch, nearly halving the bureaucracy. Since the principal source of federal spending was defense, he carried out what he called a "chaste reformation" of the armed forces. He reduced the army to three regiments totaling 3,300 officers and men strung out along the western frontier, and he devastated the navy. He ordered all six frigates confined to port and mothballed naval vessels under construction. The military academy, with a small corps of engineers, that he persuaded Congress to create at West Point received minimal funding. These measures contributed to a more constrained government, but they rested on the risky assumption that, in an age of Anglo-French depredations, the United States would not need armed strength but could get by with militia and a "mosquito" flotilla of vulnerable gunboats. The president also shut the US embassies in Holland, Portugal, and Prussia.

By eliminating the internal revenue service, Jefferson got rid of five hundred employees in the empire Hamilton had built at the Treasury, but he could not undo all that Hamilton had wrought. Gallatin even expanded the realm of the Bank of the United States. Early in 1802, Jefferson confided, "When this government was first established, it was possible to have set it going on true principles, but the contracted, half-lettered ideas of Hamilton destroyed that hope in the bud. . . . We can never get rid of his financial system. It mortifies me to be strengthening principles which I deem radically vicious, but this vice is entailed on us by the first error."

Much of the retrenchment disadvantaged Federalist officeholders. Jefferson started out by saying that he did not intend to replace "good men, to whom there is no objection but a difference of political principle" and who, in voting Federalist, were merely exercising "the right of a private citizen." There were limits, however, to his forbearance. In his inaugural address, he uttered the memorable sentence, "We are all republicans, we are all federalists," but he did not capitalize "federalists." Three days later, he confided that hardcore Federalists "I abandon as incurables, & will never turn an inch out of my way to reconcile." He even said that he wanted to "sink federalism into an abyss from which there shall be no resurrection." At the outset, though, he expressed the desire to absorb "well-meaning" Federalists in the Republican fold in accord with the "ancient Whig principles" of 1776. He had only contempt, however, for "the heretical sect of monarchists," whom he called "those pitiable maniacs." He ousted Federalist marshals and district attorneys, though not speedily enough for some partisans. If rewarding Republicans with slots held by Federalists "should not be the case," one party warrior asked, "for what, in the name of God, have we been contending?"

Jefferson came to share this view—to such an extent, some critics claim, that the spoils system, usually identified with Andrew Jackson, actually began with the third president. When New Haven merchants castigated him for ousting a Federalist customs collector who had been a midnight appointee, Jefferson raised a series of questions in rebuttal: "Is it *political intolerance* to claim a proportionate share in the direction of the public affairs? . . . If a due participation of office is a matter of right, how are vacancies to be obtained? Those by death are few; by resignation, none. Can any other mode than that of removal be proposed?" Discharging employees was painful, he said, but it was his duty, and he planned to meet it. A "proportionate share," Jefferson eventually decided, meant not fifty-fifty but a percentage congruent with political allegiances in the country—more like three-quarters for Republicans. The voters who had elected him, he reasoned, expected that he would have officials who would carry out his policy objectives. In a state such as incorrigibly Federalist Connecticut, Jefferson observed, "a general sweep seems to be called for."

Though Jefferson sought to diminish the national government, he held an expansive view of the role of the president. "His Republican or Whig theories called for deference to Congress and for suspicion of executive power," the political scientist Thomas Cronin has observed. "But . . . as president he appears to have believed that the Republic, at a crucial stage of growth, demanded strong executive leadership." Jefferson took seriously his responsibility as chief magistrate. He wrote all of his state papers and, in his own hand, answered the mail he received. "It keeps me from 10 to 12 to 13 hours a day at my writing table, giving me an interval of 4 hours for riding, dining and a little unbending," he said. He insisted that each day his department heads send him all the letters that had come to them, as well as drafts of their replies. Only a president, Jefferson maintained, can "command a view of the whole ground." At one point, the secretary of the Navy, who advocated a particular bill, said, "Nay I, even I, did not dare to bring forward the measure until I had first obtained his approbation." Furthermore, Jefferson governed not in the style of a disinterested patriot-king but of a party sachem drawing upon popular support to act in the people's interest. "Jefferson," asserted the biographer Merrill Peterson, "dominated his administration more completely than Washington had done. There was rarely any doubt, in cabinet, in Congress, in the public mind, who was master."

Departing from the credo of orthodox Republicans, who were legislative supremacists, Jefferson intervened energetically in Congress to ensure the success of his program. In contrast to his Federalist predecessors, he did not believe that respect for the principle of separation of powers required abstinence from the legislative process. He and his department heads drafted bills, conferred with Congressional leaders, and discreetly lobbied for administration measures. At a time when members of Congress had no staff and no office space other than their desks on the floors of the chambers, they depended on the executive branch for information. However much he deplored parties, Jefferson, as chief legislator, counted on Republicans in both houses of Congress to advance his desires. He benefited from his party's success at the polls, as the 17–15 edge at the start of his tenure swelled to 28–6.

In entertaining groups of congressmen at elegant dinners, Jefferson spent a sum larger than his entire salary. Men who usually had to make do with boardinghouse grub were treated to sumptuous Continental feasts, prepared by the president's French *chef de cuisine* and served with the finest of wines. Dinner, reported one guest "was excellent, cooked rather in the French style (larded venison), the dessert was profuse and extremely elegant. . . . Wine in great variety, from sherry to champagne, and a few decanters of rare Spanish wine." To encourage free exchange of ideas, Jefferson seated his guests at an oval table, where he would not have place of precedence. To ensure confidentiality, he dismissed the servants and dished out the meals himself, using one of his many clever inventions, the dumbwaiter, to fetch hot food from kitchen to table. Invitations to these affairs, printed with no insignia, began not "The President requests," but "Th: Jefferson requests." He did not raise legislative matters, but Federalists were awed. "You can never be an hour in this man's company without something of the marvelous," John Quincy Adams once said, and another Federalist reported, "No one can know Mr. Jefferson and be his personal enemy."

✤✦

Jefferson believed that foreign affairs were "executive altogether," as his policy toward the piratical countries on the Barbary Coast revealed. Jefferson fully understood what he was up against. Years before, he had asked a Moroccan official why his country thought it had the right "to make war upon Nations who had done them no injury." Jefferson recorded: "The Ambassador answered . . . that it was founded on the Laws of their Prophet, that it was written in their Koran, that all nations who should not have acknowledged their authority were sinners, that it was their right and duty to make war upon them whenever they could be found, and to make slaves of all they could take as Prisoners, and that every Musselman who should be slain in battle was sure to go to Paradise."

Washington and Adams had calculated that it cost less to pay tribute than to mount armed resistance, but Jefferson resolved to fight, though only by observing constitutional scruples. When word reached him that Tripoli had signaled that it was at war with the United States by chopping down the flagpole at the US consulate and, in addition, that cruisers of the pasha of Tripoli were attacking American ships in the Mediterranean and demanding tribute, he drew upon his powers as commander in chief to assemble a naval squadron in Norfolk. But before sending it to North Africa, he sought the "approbation" of his cabinet. Even after he had ordered the flotilla to cross the Atlantic to "protect our commerce and chastise their insolence," he punctiliously observed limits by asking Congress for guidance because a president was "unauthorized by the Constitution, without the sanction of Congress, to go beyond the line of defense," since Congress alone has the power to declare war. (It took a while for Congress to oblige him with "An Act for the protection of the Commerce and Seamen of the United States against Tripolitan Corsairs.") Only after

he had gained approval did the US fleet get the go-ahead for offensive action in the Mediterranean. "The campaign against the Barbary
pirates was perfect," Joseph Ellis has maintained. "It was a safe and
limited projection of American power abroad, it displayed Jefferson's
resolve as president, it produced convenient heroes to celebrate and it
cost very little. It was . . . the ideal miniature war for Jefferson's minimalist presidency."

In 1805, after sustaining a number of setbacks at sea, Tripoli agreed
to exempt the United States from extortion, though Jefferson did
have to ransom prisoners of war, and America continued to shell out
huge sums to pay tribute to the other Barbary states. In addition,
Secretary Madison was required to supply a prostitute to the Tunisian
envoy, Sidi Suliman Mellimelli, when he came to the US capital.
Jefferson had to cope with more than one blundering commander,
but the conflict also gave the republic new tales of heroism for its annals. Admiral Horatio Nelson called a brilliant and courageous exploit
by Lieutenant Stephen Decatur in Tripoli harbor "the most bold and
daring act of the age." Gratified by the success of the Barbary ventures,
Jefferson, however, did not see them as the forerunners of imperial
initiatives. He enunciated instead a policy of cordial relations with all
nations, "entangling alliances with none."

Foreign relations provided the greatest test of Jefferson's conception of constitutional limits in an altogether unexpected fashion.
The president understood that for the vast hinterland beyond the
Alleghenies there was "on the globe one single spot, the possessor of
which is our natural and habitual enemy." If a European power closed
off New Orleans, it would deny farmers in the Ohio and Mississippi
valleys access to the Gulf of Mexico and hence to the transoceanic
world. When Spain and, more alarmingly, France raised that threat,
Jefferson sought to purchase New Orleans. At first, he was rebuffed,
but Jefferson moved adroitly by threatening to forge an alliance with
Great Britain against France. His envoy, James Monroe, let the French
know that, if they did not agree to a deal, he was instructed to move
on to London. In addition, Jefferson ordered a military offensive to

seize New Orleans. He got an unexpected advantage when a French expedition to Santo Domingue, which was envisioned as a stepping-stone to New Orleans, ended in a bloodbath. A fierce slave rebellion and ravaging yellow fever that took the lives of more than ten thousand French soldiers and the army commander, Napoleon's brother-in-law, denied France the island's sugar and coffee. "Damn sugar!" Napoleon cried. "Damn coffee, damn colonies!"

Jefferson revealed his own racist response to this uprising. When President Adams had sought to aid the insurrection leader Toussaint Louverture, who created the Republic of Haiti, Jefferson had questioned the wisdom of dealing with "rebellious Negroes." Next thing you know, he said, there would be "black crews" advancing into "Southern states." When he became president, he supported Napoleon's ambition to restore French rule and reimpose slavery on the island. "Nothing would be easier for us," Jefferson told the French envoy to the United States, "than to provide your army and fleet with everything you need, and thus reduce Toussaint to starvation." It need also be noted, however, that Jefferson, who had a way of compartmentalizing his thoughts, would go on to call upon Congress to halt the importation of slaves to America, ending "all further participation in those violations of human rights . . . on the unoffending inhabitants of Africa," and Congress complied.

In April 1803, Talleyrand, the French foreign minister, stunned a US envoy by telling him that Napoleon, fed up with the Santo Domingue venture, was willing to sell not merely New Orleans but all of "Louisiana," a territory of imprecise boundaries but conceivably encompassing every inch of the vast Mississippi and Missouri basins west to the Continental Divide. Napoleon, badly in need of cash, had more than enough to occupy him in Europe. "They ask of me only one town in Louisiana," he said, "but I already consider the colony as entirely lost." Without authorization, American agents signed a treaty to buy an empire that would double the national domain at a cost of three cents an acre. "You have made a noble bargain for yourselves, and I suppose you will make the most of it,"

Talleyrand remarked. "The Louisiana Purchase," Joseph Ellis has asserted, "was the most consequential executive decision in American history, rivaled only by Harry Truman's decision to drop the atomic bomb in 1945."

The treaty, however, presented Jefferson with a predicament. He was not troubled that the Americans in Paris had acted boldly, for they could hardly turn down such an offer, and, despite his belief in a lean budget, he was not bothered by the expenditure of millions of dollars because he was thrilled at the boundless opportunity to create a vast pastoral paradise. There was, though, another weighty objection. "The general government has no powers but such as the constitution has given it," he said, "and it has not given it a power of holding foreign territory, and still less of incorporating it into the Union." Hence, he drew up a constitutional amendment which he maintained would have to be ratified before the Senate could act on the treaty. This process, however, would be so time-consuming, he was warned, that Napoleon could renege or domestic critics might organize themselves to forestall the agreement. So he quieted his scruples. "The less we say about constitutional difficulties . . . , the better," he remarked, observing that it would be best to proceed "sub silentio."

An inveterate strict constructionist, Jefferson recognized that he had engaged in a momentous departure from the true faith. "Our peculiar security is in possession of a written Constitution," he commented. "Let us not make it a blank paper by construction." He acknowledged that "the Executive in seizing the fugitive occurrence which so much advances the good of their country have done an act beyond the Constitution" and reflected that "the Legislature" would be "casting behind them metaphysical subtleties." When Congress subsequently granted Jefferson, at his request, plenary authority over the Louisiana Territory that has been likened to that exercised earlier in North America by George III, John Quincy Adams observed that there was "an assumption of implied powers greater than all the assumptions of implied powers in the years of the Washington and Adams administrations put together." In his diary, JQA set down this analysis:

The Louisiana purchase was in substance a dissolution and re-composition of the whole Union. It made a Union totally different from that for which the Constitution had been formed. It gives despotic powers over the territories purchased. . . . It makes French and Spanish Laws a part of the Laws of the Union. It introduces whole systems of Legislation abhorrent to the Spirit and character of our Institutions, and all this done by an Administration which came in blowing Trumpet against implied powers.

For Jefferson, Joyce Appleby has maintained, the land of the Louisiana Purchase represented "an empire of liberty, white men's liberty, . . . a tabula rasa for the American Adam, that self-sufficient, liberty-loving, energetic innovator supported by his independent family. He and his ilk would carry the plow, the church, the schoolroom, and the court-house into the fertile land that had heretofore been the haunts of savages."

No one could gainsay the magnificence of Jefferson's acquisition. The nearly one million square miles constituted the greatest parcel of land ever transferred from one nation state to another, a territory larger than Great Britain, Germany, France, Spain, and Portugal combined. It gave the young republic prodigious mountains of ore and made possible "amber fields of grain" that would become the bread-basket of the world. It also, though, added to the United States a vast expanse into which slavery could spread and Indians could be moved. After drafting a document that articulated the rights of "the inhabit-ants" of Louisiana, Jefferson altered it to "*white* inhabitants."

Shortly after acquiring Louisiana, Jefferson sent his private secretary, Meriwether Lewis, with co-leader William Clark, on an ambitious exploration of the trans-Mississippi west. The expedition appeared to result directly from the cession of the new territory, but Jefferson had planned it long before he had any idea Louisiana might be for sale. He was proposing to send the men into what was then a foreign land. His only doubt was whether his constitutional powers extended to initiating a reconnaissance motivated primarily by scientific curiosity. Hence, in asking for Congressional approval, he disingenuously em-phasized the benefits to interstate commerce of charting a route of

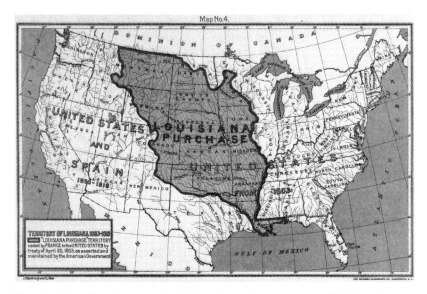

The Louisiana Purchase, acquired from France in 1803, compelled Americans
in the original Atlantic seaboard states to re-envision the topography of their
country, for the added territory embraced not only Louisiana but also a wide
swath of land to the northwest extending to the eastern edge of what would
become the state of Idaho. *Records of the Bureau of Land Management, Record
Group 49; National Archives, National Archives Identifier*

navigation from the Missouri valley to the Pacific, while remarking
offhandedly that the prospect that the Corps of Discovery might "in-
cidentally advance the geographical knowledge of our own continent
can not but be an additional gratification." In fact, Jefferson arranged
to have Lewis tutored by renowned scholars in subjects such as botany,
and at Monticello the president himself taught his secretary celestial
navigation. Jefferson gave him minute instructions, too, on what he
should observe, including "the dates at which particular plants put
forth or lose their flower, or leaf" as well as "times of appearances of
particular birds, reptiles or insects."

Jubilation over the acquisition of Louisiana permitted Jefferson to
enter the 1804 campaign with a record of almost uninterrupted success. The Republican caucus in Congress underscored his popularity
by renominating him unanimously. Tall, slender, with flecks of red
in his graying hair, Thomas Jefferson was an attractive candidate. So

feeble had the Federalists become in the brief period since Adams's narrow defeat that Jefferson won 92 percent of the electoral vote, crushing his Federalist rival by taking every state but Connecticut and Delaware. Each of the states he won, he carried unanimously in the Electoral College save for a couple of Maryland defectors. Jefferson saw his triumph as yet another endorsement of the Patriot cause. "We entered young into the first revolution and saw it terminate happily," he said. "We had to engage when old in a second more perilous, because our people were divided. But we have weathered this too and seen all come round and to rights."

In truth, not all came round. In the month after the election, "A Friend of the Constitution" informed the president, "There is a plan to murder you. . . . A band of hardy fellows have joined to do it. They are to carry daggers and pistols. I have been invited to join them but would rather suffer death. I advise you to take care . . . how you walk about as some of the assassins are already in Washington." Another message alerted him: "Julius Caesar was cautioned for the Ides of March—I caution you for the last of April." There was, however, never an attempt on Jefferson's life.

The country no longer had Aaron Burr as vice president because of an encounter earlier in that election year. In June 1804, Burr challenged Hamilton to a duel, and the former secretary of the treasury agreed to meet him on a field of honor. Since New York punished dueling, the two men were rowed across the Hudson to Weehawken, New Jersey, where they drew weapons on a ledge of the Palisades above the river. A bullet from Burr's gun penetrated deeply. A physician said of Hamilton: "His countenance of death I shall never forget. He had at that instant strength to say, 'This is a mortal wound, Doctor.'" A few days later, Alexander Hamilton died. Though both men's lives were at risk, a pro-Hamilton newspaper called Burr a "BASE ASSASSIN," and a New Jersey grand jury indicted him for murder. When the 1804 Republican caucus took up the vice presidential slot, a congressman reported, "Mr. Burr had not one single vote, and not a word was lisped in his favor."

➤◄

Jefferson's second term, which began so auspiciously with his huge election victory, ended miserably, conspicuously in his continuing struggles with the federal judiciary. "Whereas in his first term," the biographer R. B. Bernstein has written, "he had showed initiative, creativity, and flexibility, regularly seizing opportunities to direct events, in his second term he was, rather, reacting to events, while displaying tendencies of dogmatism, intolerance, and rigidity." Jefferson created a huge controversy by instigating the sensational impeachment trial of a US Supreme Court justice. For years, Samuel Chase had disgraced himself and the tribunal by using the bench as a political platform for harangues against democracy, notoriously in his outrageous conduct of sedition trials. In May 1803, Chase went too far. "You must have heard of the extraordinary charge of Chase to the Grand Jury at Baltimore," Jefferson wrote a Maryland congressman. "Ought this . . . attack on the principles of our Constitution, and on the proceedings of a State, to go unpunished?" The House of Representatives took a while to respond to Jefferson's prod, but, after a time, it voted 73–32 to impeach the Federalist judge. Not enough Republicans, however, were convinced that Chase's tirades, though abominable, constituted "high crimes and misdemeanors," and Jefferson himself stayed aloof from the proceedings. On March 1, 1805, a majority of the Senate voted to oust Chase, but it did not muster the stipulated two-thirds requirement, and only rarely thereafter have presidents contemplated impeachment as a feasible weapon for disciplining misbehaving judges.

Aaron Burr embroiled Jefferson in a considerably more ominous court procedure. The skullduggery of the president's former associate beggars belief. While vice president of the United States, Burr had offered his services to Great Britain, as he later would to Spain, in a nefarious plot. The British minister reported to London that Burr was eager "to lend his assistance to His Majesty's Government in any Manner in which they may think fit to employ him, particularly in endeavouring to effect a Separation of the Western Part of the United States from that which lies between the Atlantick and the Mountains."

(Authorities in Madrid were informed that Burr planned to capture Washington, DC, and assassinate the president, whose body would be thrown into the Potomac.) Though scholars disagree about the precise nature of the Burr conspiracy, the foremost early authority, Thomas Perkins Abernethy, concluded that "next to the Confederate War it posed the greatest threat of dismemberment which the American Union has ever faced."

In the fall of 1806, Jefferson learned that Burr had been spotted at the head of a flotilla of armed men descending the Ohio River, apparently with the bizarre intent of attacking Mexico, along perhaps with detaching the American West to create a new empire. He ordered their capture and then orchestrated the trial of Burr, charged under the treason clause with "levying war" against the United States. In an ill-advised message to Congress, the president said that Burr's "guilt is placed beyond question." As John Adams rightly commented, "If his guilt is as clear as the Noon day Sun, the first Magistrate ought not to have pronounced it so before a Jury had tryed him."

Once again, Jefferson clashed with his nemesis, John Marshall, who presided over the trial in Richmond. When Burr requested the court to subpoena Jefferson, the president balked. "Would the Executive be independent of the Judiciary if he were subject to the *commands* of the latter, & to imprisonment for disobedience; if the several courts could bandy him from pillar to post, keep him constantly trudging from North to South & East to West, and withdraw him entirely from his constitutional duties?" he asked. Jefferson also threw a cloak of immunity over his subordinates. But he did provide all the documents sought, and neither Burr nor Marshall insisted on his appearance. The chief justice, however, showed partiality in attending a dinner where Burr and his lawyer were guests. In addition, he defined "levying war" so strictly that, much to the president's disappointment, he rejected the felony charge of treason, although he did approve a misdemeanor charge of launching an expedition against Mexico. The jury wound up setting Burr free. Jefferson accused Marshall of twisting "Burr's neck out of the halter of treason." But, he concluded, "On the whole, this squall, by showing with what ease our government suppresses movements which in other countries require armies, has greatly increased its strength by increasing the public confidence in it."

+-+

Far more than the Burr conspiracy, maritime afflictions devoured Jefferson's second term and showed him in the least favorable light. Confronted with the grievous challenge of British depredations on American commerce during the Napoleonic wars, Jefferson piloted the ship of state with uncertain hand. At times, he was so passive that he provided no leadership at all. On other occasions, he was so bellicose that his cabinet officials had to restrain him. Moreover, Jefferson, often thought of as a pacifist, nursed dreams of empire. When in 1807 war with Britain seemed unavoidable, he told his secretary of state, "I had rather have war against Spain than not, if we go to war against England. Our Southern defensive force can take the Floridas, volunteers for a Mexican army will flock to our standard, & rich pabulum will be offered to our privateers in the plunder of their commerce & coasts." He added, "Probably Cuba would add itself to our confederation," a goal both of imperialists and of slave owners—then, and for decades to come.

In trying to cope with incursions at sea, the president had several options, none of them palatable. He could avoid danger to Americans on the ocean and conflict with the British by keeping US vessels in port. To do so would be to cut off American merchants from an extraordinarily lucrative trade. The value of US exports, $2 million in 1790, soared to $108 million in 1807, and the tonnage carried by ships under the American flag in this period would not be surpassed in more than a century. A second course was to build military and naval strength to a level that would gain the respect of other powers. But that would take time, run counter to the president's loathing of standing armies and costly navies, and enormously dilate federal expenditures. Perhaps the best policy was to allow American maritime interests to continue to take risks and hope for an early end to the European war. Jefferson might at the same time try diplomacy to gain whatever respect for neutral rights the British could be persuaded to grant. But when two US envoys negotiated a pact, Jefferson, angry that the terms did not go far enough to meet his demands, refused to send it to the Senate.

Never could Jefferson bring himself to look at the predicament through British eyes. After the battle of Austerlitz, Napoleon, having knocked Austria out of the war and sent the Russians reeling, was, as Jefferson acknowledged, "bestriding the continent of Europe like a Colossus." For the British, their very survival depended on taking advantage of supremacy on the seas to deny France vital supplies. Consequently, no responsible leader in London could put his country in jeopardy by permitting Americans to perforate their blockade in order to profit from sales to the French.

Nor did Whitehall comprehend the US perception. As Gordon Wood has elucidated, "It was not the actual number of seizures that most irritated Americans; rather it was the British presumption that His Majesty's government had the right to decide just what American trade should be permitted or not permitted. It seemed to reduce America once again to the status of a colonial dependent. This was the fundamental issue that underlay America's turbulent relationship with Britain through the entire period of the European wars." Impressment, too, reflected the refusal of Whitehall to accept the authority of the United States as a sovereign nation to enact naturalization statutes that would transmute British subjects into American citizens. One contemptuous British diplomat said of Americans: "We drove them into being a nation when they were no more fit for it than the convicts of Botany Bay."

Jefferson believed that in dealing with British transgressions the United States had three choices—war, embargo, or capitulation—but in a special message to Congress in January 1806 he abstained from making any recommendation, to the dismay of his critics. "It is not for the master and mate . . . in bad weather to go below, and leave the management of the ship to the cook and cabin boy," sniped the pesky gadfly, John Randolph, but Jefferson, strangely, remained detached.

Left to its own devices, Congress enacted a non-intercourse law banning the importation of specified British goods. Jefferson indicated
that he looked favorably on the action, which he had done nothing
to promote.

In June 1807, the two countries approached the precipice of war
when the HMS *Leopard* fired broadsides at close range toward a US
naval vessel, the frigate *Chesapeake*, off the Virginia Capes, killing
or wounding twenty-one sailors; forcing the Americans to strike
the stars and stripes; and, after boarding, removing four seamen the
British claimed were deserters from the Royal Navy. Though the
Crown had long regarded American merchantmen as fair game, they
had never before assaulted a ship of the US fleet. Jefferson demanded
redress for this affront to national sovereignty, including return of
the four men and a pledge to abandon the practice of impressment,
but, with war fever running high, he held off calling Congress into
special session exceptionally early which would permit it to declare
war when fevers were hot. He did, however, order British warships
to depart from US harbors and took steps to rearm, though primarily
by adding to the number of gunboats, which were chiefly of use
on the coast, not the high seas. Even when disturbing news arrived
that Britain had court-martialed the four; hanged one of them; and
subjected each of the other three sailors, who were American-born,
to five hundred lashes, Jefferson would do nothing that might compromise the constitutional authority of Congress to decide for or
against war.

Yet he also advanced bold claims to executive prerogative when he
spent money for munitions that Congress had not appropriated. "To
have awaited a previous & special sanction by law would have lost occasions which might not be retrieved," he told Congress later. "I trust
that the Legislature . . . will approve, when done, what they would
have seen so important to be done if then assembled." That same
year, he wrote, "On great occasions, every good officer must be ready
to risk himself in going beyond the strict line of the law, when the
public preservation requires it." He then advanced the problematic

claim, "His motives will be a justification." Three years later, Jefferson asserted, "A strict observance of the written laws is doubtless one of the highest duties of a good citizen, but it is not *the highest*. The laws of necessity, of self-preservation, of saving our country when in danger, are of a higher obligation. To lose our country by a scrupulous adherence to written law would be to lose the law itself, with life, liberty, property & all those who are enjoying them with us; thus absurdly sacrificing the ends to the means."

Six months after the assault on the *Chesapeake*, Congress, at Jefferson's request, mandated a total maritime embargo, forbidding US ships to sail to foreign ports and foreign vessels to load and unload cargo in America. The United States, Jefferson contended, must insulate itself from "the present paroxysm of the insanity of Europe." Commercial retaliation did not coerce the British to relent, though it hurt them some and their Caribbean possessions considerably more. By ordering US ships to remain at anchor, Jefferson hoped to eliminate conflicts at sea that could ignite a war. The embargo, intended as a temporary measure, lasted fifteen months—the remainder of Jefferson's presidency—with devastating effects. The value of US exports plunged from $108 million in 1807 to $22 million in 1808. Merchants went broke, ships rotted in harbor, longshoremen were unemployed, and beached sailors peered despondently at the sea. Both Portland, Maine, and Newburyport, Massachusetts, had to set up soup kitchens to sustain the idled, and in the bustling shipbuilding harbor of Bath, Maine, forty-three vessels heard no call to venture out. Wiscasset, Maine, sent off sixty-seven cargoes in 1807, just two the next year. At a time when the tariff was the biggest source of revenue for the young republic, customs receipts vanished. In the South, planters were deprived of markets for their crops. The actions of the British and the French combined had not wrought as much damage as the blockade the United States imposed on itself.

As chief enforcer of the embargo, Jefferson wound up violating his most cherished principles. Dumas Malone later concluded that Jefferson became "so obsessed with . . . making the embargo work as to be unmindful of republican theory and also of certain basic facts of human nature." When Americans sought to evade the embargo, Jefferson took punitive action far exceeding infractions of civil liberties by the Federalists earlier. Secretary Gallatin counseled that "dangerous and odious" methods were required, and Jefferson instructed Congress to "legalize all *means* which may be necessary to obtain its *end*."

Unchastened by rebukes from his own appointees to the US Supreme Court, Jefferson adopted extreme measures that violated the Fourth Amendment's protection against unreasonable searches and seizures; employed the army and navy to execute arbitrary edicts; and even resorted to prosecutions for treason. He viewed the rafting of goods by smugglers across Lake Champlain to Canada as an insurrection that he ordered put down by militias. To be sure, most citizens were law-abiding, but in the Lake Champlain and Passamaquoddy regions, smugglers fired shots at government officials. In his path-breaking study, Leonard Levy asserted, "On a prolonged, widespread, and systematic basis, . . . the armed forces harried and beleaguered the citizenry." In vain did a Madisonian publication contrast the "temporary inconvenience" of the embargo with what would be the consequences of war: "loss of millions of dollars, burning and sacking of towns and cities, rape, theft, murders, streams of blood, weeping widows, helpless orphans, the beggary of thousands."

As a consequence, critics upbraided Jefferson. "You infernal villain," a Boston man wrote him. "How much longer are you going to keep this damned Embargo on to starve us poor people. One of my children has already starved to death of which I am ashamed and declared that it died of an apoplexy. I have three more children which I expect will die soon if I don't get something for them to eat which cannot be had." At age thirteen, William Cullen Bryant, later to be celebrated as one of America's greatest poets, began a screed by writing, "Go, wretch, resign the presidential chair," and went on to urge him to "sink supinely in . . . sable arms" and "quit to abler hands the helm of state."

Another of Jefferson's outraged constituents who called on the president to abandon the embargo said, "Damn my eyes if I can live as it is." He continued:

> I shall certainly cut my throat, and if I do you will lose one of the best seamen that ever sailed. I have a wife and four young ones to support, and it goes damn'd hard with me now. If I don't cut my throat, I will go into the English and fight against you. I hope, honored Sir, you will forgive the abrupt manner in which this is wrote as I am damn'd mad. But still, if I ever catch you . . . , take care of your honored neck.

The sailor signed his name to the threatening letter and appended his address (No. 9 Pine St.), saying, "If you want to see him, you damn'd rascal."

With the embargo a dreadful failure, and no acceptable substitute available, Jefferson went into full retreat. He had already decided against seeking another term, citing "the sound precedent set by an illustrious predecessor." By invoking Washington, he appeared to be sacrificing his own career in order to solidify the two-term tradition. In truth, he regarded his tenure as the source of "nothing but unceasing drudgery and daily loss of friends." He also confided as the sands ran down,

> Never did a prisoner released from his chains feel such relief as I shall on shaking off the shackles of power. Nature intended me for the tranquil pursuits of science, by rendering them my supreme delight. But the enormities of the time in which I have lived have forced me . . . to commit myself to the boisterous ocean of political passions. I thank God for the opportunity of retiring from them without censure, and carrying with me the more consoling proofs of public approbation.

With the option of another term closed, he was content to wait out his remaining months inertly, an "unmeddling listener to what others say." Jefferson's withdrawal disconcerted his cabinet. Both Vice President Madison and Secretary Gallatin pleaded with him to offer some direction. As Gallatin said, with regard to choosing between war and continuing the embargo, "I think that we must (or rather you must) decide the question absolutely, so that we may point out a decisive course either way to our friends."

Jefferson would not heed. "The President gives no opinion as to the measures that ought to be adopted," one of his congressional leaders remarked. "It is not known whether he be for war or peace." In his final State of the Union message in November 1808, Jefferson requested Congress "to weigh . . . the painful alternatives out of which choice is to be made," but declined to make any recommendation. "I think it is fair," he said, "to leave to those who are to act on them the decisions they prefer, being . . . myself but a spectator." And it was as "a spectator" that Thomas Jefferson ended his presidency.

⊹⊱

When Jefferson's term drew to a close in March 1809, the *National Intelligencer* paid him this tribute: "Never will it be forgotten as long as liberty is dear to man that it was on this day that Thomas Jefferson retired from the supreme magistracy amidst the blessings and regrets of Millions." This is a judgment that has been echoed through the years. In 1874, his early biographer James Parton asserted, "If Jefferson was wrong, America is wrong. If America is right, Jefferson was right." Decades later, Woodrow Wilson declared, "Jefferson's principles are sources of light because they are not made up of pure reason, but spring out of aspiration, impulse, vision, sympathy. They burn with the fervor of the heart." More recently, the biographer Jon Meacham has maintained, "Jefferson speaks to us now because he spoke so powerfully and creatively to us then."

Not all twenty-first-century scholars, however, are willing to embrace Jefferson as a model for addressing contemporary problems. They acknowledge the power of his rhetoric in the Declaration of Independence and his first inaugural address but also underscore his biases. "Historians," Jeffrey Pasley has reported, "have given readers a cloistered rural intellectual who hoped that America could long remain a prosperous agricultural backwater and a proudly southern politico whose cant masked a deep devotion to protecting his region's parochial interests, including slavery." Some of his statements and actions do raise doubts about whether he truly believed that "all" are endowed with rights.

Numerous comments by Jefferson make evident that he was a racist. "Blacks," he said bluntly, "are inferior to whites in the endowments of both mind and body." He also found them repellent because, he said, they exuded a foul odor. When women of color such as the poet Phillis Wheatley demonstrated mental acuity, he belittled them. Jefferson also expressed horror at racial amalgamation that would defile white blood at the same time that he continued his sexual liaison with his slave Sally Hemings, who bore him more than one child.

To be sure, Jefferson denounced slavery, but, as Joyce Appleby remarked, he "backed away from attacking the institution as his power to do something about it increased." In his autobiography, Jefferson stated, "Nothing is more certainly written in the book of fate than that these people are to be free." In his *Notes on the State of Virginia*, he observed, "Indeed I tremble for my country when I reflect that God is just, that his justice cannot sleep forever." But when a young Virginian revealed that he was contemplating emancipating his slaves, Jefferson warned him against doing so since blacks and whites could not share the same land. Jefferson was also capable of advising a nephew, "I consider a woman who brings a child every two years more profitable than the best man on the farm. What she produces is an addition to the capital, while his labors disappear in mere consumption."

An apostle of liberty, Jefferson fell short in his treatment of Native Americans, too, though he greatly admired them and was sensitive to their plight. "Endowed with the faculties and rights of men, breathing an ardent love of liberty and independence, and occupying a country which left them no desire but to be undisturbed," Jefferson said, "they have been overwhelmed by the current, or driven before it." But, when governor of Virginia, he had instructed George Rogers Clark that "against these Indians, the end proposed should be their extermination, or their removal beyond the lakes of Illinois river; the same world will scarcely do for them and us." Later, when president, he told his secretary of war that Shawnee chieftains should be informed that if the US government were to "lift the hatchet against any tribe, we will never lay it down till the tribe is exterminated, or driven beyond the Mississippi." Gordon Wood has concluded, "The Jefferson that emerges out of much recent scholarship therefore resembles the America many critics have visualized over the past three decades—self-righteous, guilt-ridden, racist, doctrinaire, and filled with liberal pieties that under stress are easily sacrificed."

Numbers of scholars, however, maintain that Jefferson, though undeniably flawed, was a democrat who waged a pitched battle against elite rule. Brian Steele has stressed the third president's "willingness to trust the political and moral instincts of the American public . . . in a way that few political theorists before or since have done." Marc Landy and Sidney Milkis have called Jefferson "the first committed democrat to preside over America," and Richard Ellis contends that "Jeffersonian Democracy" is best understood "as the final phase of the American Revolution." John Ferling notes that "the great majority of those who were alive in 1826 recognized Jefferson's achievements in breaking many of the fetters that had existed before 1776." Jeffrey Pasley, too, maintains that "the movement and party Jefferson headed were steeped in Enlightenment liberalism and democratic radicalism." Joyce Appleby has declared that Jefferson "resisted the notion that political equality was a chimera and strove to root out the last monarchical remnants from American culture," work that "put him at odds with the country's privileged upper class and especially its political arm, the Federalist party."

Appleby points out that in the last letter Jefferson ever wrote he expressed pleasure at the revelation of the palpable truth "that the mass of mankind has not been born with saddles on their backs, nor a favored few booted and spurred, ready to ride them legitimately, by the grace of God." Strange words, she acknowledges, to come from a patrician slave owner. But Appleby concludes: "It would be a grave error of historical judgment to underestimate the significance of Jefferson's successful assault on the venerable dogma of natural inequality that was based on the belief that most men and women were created to be the hewers of wood and drawers of water for the 'favored few.'"

In truth, Thomas Jefferson is an elusive figure. Writing about him in the nineteenth century, Henry Adams commented, "Almost every other American statesman might be described in a parenthesis. A few broad strokes of the brush would paint the portraits of all the early Presidents with this exception, . . . Jefferson could be painted only touch by touch, with a fine pencil, and the perfection of the likeness depended upon the shifting and uncertain flicker of its semi-transparent shadows." In the modern era, Merrill Peterson, after devoting three decades to research and writing on the Sage of Monticello, offered the "mortifying confession" that "Jefferson remains for me, finally, an impenetrable man." Much of the difficulty derives from the fact that Jefferson made statements that could not be given credence but that he convinced himself were true. "Jefferson," observed the historian Bernard Bailyn, "would, if need be, jump out of a syllogism to save the major premise."

But generations after his death Americans continue to care about Jefferson—to school themselves on what he did, to understand what he portended. "We are continually asking ourselves," Gordon Wood has written, "whether Jefferson still survives, or what is still living in the thought of Jefferson. . . . No figure in our history has embodied so much of our heritage and so many of our hopes." No one would have been so little surprised by this preoccupation than Thomas Jefferson. He imagined that on some future July 4 the writing desk on which he composed the Declaration of Independence might be "carried in the procession of our nation's birthday, as the relics of the saints are in those of the church." An episode somewhat like that occurred when, on April 13, 1943, five thousand people watched President Franklin Delano Roosevelt dedicate the Thomas Jefferson Memorial in the capital's cherry-blossomed Tidal Basin. In the pages of *The Saturday Review*, Dumas Malone reflected that the erection of the building "signifies in a tangible way his recognition as a member of our Trinity of immortals." Jefferson, historians Scot French and Edward Ayers announced, "had finally joined George Washington and Abraham Lincoln in the pantheon of American demigods."

Mention of Franklin D. Roosevelt, however, focuses attention on how contested Jefferson's legacy is. In the New Deal era, FDR and his liberal supporters hailed Jefferson as the founder of their party and convened at "Jefferson Day" banquets. Jefferson, Franklin Roosevelt contended, "believed, as we do, that the average opinion of mankind is in the long run superior to the dictates of the self-chosen." But as Joseph Ellis has asserted, "Roosevelt's appropriation of Jefferson as a New Deal Democrat was one of the most inspired acts of political thievery in American history, since the growth of federal power during the New Deal represented . . . the death knell for Jefferson's idea of a minimalist government." When right-wing Democrats sought to impede the re-election of FDR, their party's nominee, they called themselves "Jeffersonian Democrats."

Nothing in Jefferson's rhetoric suggests affinity with the principal theme of liberal government in the modern era. "All the progressive causes in American history—from the rights of labor to the struggles of women and ethnic minorities—required the authority of the state for their realization," John Patrick Diggins has asserted. "Ironically the egalitarian ideals Jefferson espoused would be realized in the very institutions he opposed." As early as 1787, Jefferson had written Madison, "I own I am not a friend to very energetic government." Little wonder that the historian Carl Becker concluded that Jefferson thought that "the only thing to do with political power, since it is inherently dangerous, is to abate it." Jefferson's conception, Merrill Peterson maintained, "has crippled the government and, indeed, kept it from responding to the will of the people." Consequently, in the twenty-first century Jefferson's presidency is not a usable past for a statesman seeking to defend or expand national power. Still, it is unreasonable to measure Jefferson primarily by his relevance to problems of a distant age that he could not possibly have been expected to visualize. "Jefferson isn't exactly 'ours,'" Brian Steele has declared. "The thought that animated his politics was forged in a world we have lost and cannot be assimilated to our own time or recovered pure for implementation today."

Steele has offered a wise long-range assessment of Jefferson's performance. "Instead of rejecting Jefferson's sins as somehow not American enough for us, on the one hand, or merely celebrating him by ignoring his failings," he has contended, "one might want to consider this historiographical moment (which has been largely negative for Jefferson's reputation) as an opportunity to chasten our tendency to self-congratulation and find the moral courage to face our own limitations. Instead of defending Jefferson so we can celebrate him once again, we might embrace his complexity as a way of adjusting our conception of ourselves as a nation which, as Christopher Hitchens has put it, has both 'upheld great values and principles' and 'committed gross wrongs and crimes.'"

It is outside the political arena that Jefferson remains a towering and challenging presence. As an "Olympian humanist" (Peterson's term), he has engendered essays with titles such as "Jefferson the Naturalist," "Pioneer Botanist," and "Father of American Paleontology." Writers on the origins of US scientific inquiry, Peterson reported, "encountered Jefferson at every turn." Indeed, it is easier to demonstrate that Jefferson was a great American than that he was a great president. More than one historian has noted the unexpected language of the epitaph Jefferson composed for his tomb:

> Author of the Declaration of American Independence
> of the Statute of Virginia for religious freedom
> and Father of the University of Virginia

These are the accomplishments of his lifetime he wishes "most to be remembered." He makes no mention of his eight years as president of the United States.

5

James Madison

Leading the Nation through the Perilous War of 1812

Jefferson's torpor began a period of more than twenty years of subsiding presidential power, as the tenure of his successor, James Madison, starkly disclosed. Dolley Madison, who staged the first inaugural ball, cut more of a figure in the capital than did her husband. With a turban of Parisian satin flaunting bird-of-paradise plumes topping her head and gold chains circling her ample waist, the regal First Lady, "queen of hearts," dwarfed the undersized president. Washington Irving, who described Dolley Madison as a "fine, portly, buxom dame with a good word for everybody," said, "as to Jemmy Madison—Ah! poor Jemmy!—he is but a withered little apple-john." One visitor to America, a distinguished Scottish barrister, found the short Madison to be "a little, mean-looking, yellow, cunning, sour, awkward personage, attired in proper black with a profusion of powder on his lank scanty locks and the wrinkles of his orange colored forehead."

Commentators found the James Madison who at the Philadelphia convention had earned such high regard as father of the Constitution unrecognizable in the executive office. An English diplomat who thought Jefferson "more of a statesman and man of the world than Mr. Madison" acknowledged that Madison "was better informed, and, moreover, was a social, jovial and good-humored companion full of anecdote." But an admirable comportment did not suffice. No match

Critics jeered that the fourth president was scrawny and sickly, but in this
lithograph based on a portrait by Gilbert Stuart, James Madison projects the
image of a stalwart founding father. At the culmination of the War of 1812,
Americans chose to believe that "Mister Madison's War" was a triumph, but
over the years he has gained greater esteem as "father of the Constitution."
National Portrait Gallery, Smithsonian Institution, NPG.77.89

for Jefferson as a communicator, Madison, in his inaugural address, de-livered what the political scientist Fred Greenstein has called a "mind-numbing 374-word sentence." Frequent illnesses confined Madison to bed; one especially virulent bilious fever nearly cost him his life. He often absented himself from Washington to hole up on his Virginia plan-tation. "Our President," John C. Calhoun of South Carolina confided, "tho a man of amiable manners and great talents has not I fear those commanding talents which are necessary to controul those about him."

Congress regarded Madison and other presidents of this period as beholden to it, since these heads of state had been nominated (and hence, in a period when there was no serious opposition, elected) by a congressional caucus. Cabinet members, recognizing where power lay, bypassed the chief executive and struck deals with congressional com-mittee chairmen. "James the first of America will take possession of the throne on the fourth of March," said a supercilious Federalist con-gressman at the outset. "I think Friend James will have rather a trouble-some reign." Three years later, John Randolph said of Madison, "He is President *de jure* only; who exercises the office *de facto* I do not know."

→←

Napoleon Bonaparte's wars, however, drew even Madison into the assertion of extraordinary authority at times. Madison issued one proclamation curbing Congress that his biographer Irving Brant later wrote brought to mind the action of a King in Council. Madison also seized on an opportunity after Congress had dispersed to order troops to proclaim acquisition of West Florida, which extended northwest beyond Baton Rouge, though Spain refused to abide by the proclam-ation. He did this not only without authorization but also without Congress's knowledge, since he kept his directive a secret. With even less justification, he menaced Spanish settlements such as Amelia Island off east Florida's Atlantic coast.

Like Jefferson, Madison sought to defy Britain and France while avoiding war with either. On the very day he was inaugurated, the embargo that Madison, its principal architect, had conceded was a "failure" expired. But the embargo was followed by a series of make-shifts culminating in a bill that sought to play the two powers off one another. Madison and the Republicans have been roundly criticized for failing to mount a military mobilization that would have made American threats more credible, but, in truth, it is improbable that any US policy would have been effective, so determined was Boney to prevail, so resolved were the English to safeguard their sceptered isle.

For the most part Madison temporized, leaving it to Congress to step up the tempo toward war. Led by Calhoun and Kentucky's Henry Clay, the coruscating Speaker of the House, "war hawks" derided the president's policy of peaceful coercion and demanded that he ready the army for action. "What!" Clay exclaimed, "Shall it be said that our *amor patriae* is located at these desks—that we pusillanimously cling to our seats here rather than boldly vindicate the most inestimable rights of the country?" Madison, though complaisant, hoped that he might still muddle through. But Napoleon toyed with him, and a British envoy proved no more trustworthy. Negotiations with Britain foundered after a madman gunned down the prime minister, Spencer Perceval, in the lobby of the House of Commons. A British blockade strangled American trade. When in 1812 Madison sent Congress a message reporting on indignities the British had inflicted on Americans, he added that whether the United States "shall continue passive under these progressive usurpations and these accumulating wrongs [is] a solemn question which the Constitution wisely confides to the legislative department of the Government." In that manner, the United States drifted into the War of 1812.

While Madison bided his time, Jefferson tried as best he could to reconcile himself to the eagerness of Republicans for war. He had thought that the country he had done so much to create would be exempt from this curse of the Old World. America had been intended as "a garden for the delight and multiplication of mankind," he said. "But the lions and tigers of Europe must be gorged in blood, and some of ours must go, it seems, to their maws, their ravenous and insatiable maws." Still, there was one solace. War portended "the second weaning from British principles, British attachments, British manners and manufactures," and the advent of "an epoch in the spirit of nationalism." Jefferson, however, hoped that Madison would be able to reign in peace, for, he said, "I know no government which would be so embarrassing in war as ours."

A multitude of causes impelled the United States toward war. Orders in Council resulted in the seizure of US merchant vessels, and the impressment of seamen was a persistent provocation. Accordingly, some coastal communities rallied to the cry, "Free Trade and Sailors' Rights." In the hinterland, frontiersmen accused the British of employing Indian "savages" as "hired assassins." (In its scramble toward war, the country sometimes made too much of these grievances. Shipowners created trouble for themselves by hiring deserters from the British navy, and Indian raids owed more to rapacious settlers who had Madison's support than to British conspirators.) Many Americans believed, too, that, to win international respect for the new republic, Yanks needed to give the redcoats a sound thrashing. (The United States had reason to go to war with France, too, but Madison knew better than to engage two European powers, and, as the historian Ralph Ketcham has written, Britain's "deliberate insults to American rights, in ways that required permanent economic subservience to the former mother country, made Napoleon's mere selfish, tactical depredations seem petty by comparison.")

On June 1, 1812, Madison urged Congress to declare war, though he did so mostly by implication, and he spent much of the ensuing conflict seeking to explain why he advocated war. He stubbornly insisted that an indispensable feature of any settlement was British abandonment of impressment, though there was never the remotest possibility that the Crown would do so. Furthermore, New England, which suffered most from impressment, opposed war. There appeared to be no shortage of Yankee lads willing to seek a livelihood at sea despite the risk. The president also mentioned that "the great staples of our country have been cut off from their legitimate markets," but he was wary of using a dollar sign as a justification for bloodshed. In implying that the United States would not "continue passive under these progressive usurpations," he anticipated his later contention that the United States was fighting a second war for independence—a plausible explanation because Britain was continuing to treat Americans as colonials. "In retrospect," the historian Lynn Hudson Parsons has observed, "the cause of the War of 1812 seems to have been American frustration at the refusal of major powers to take the new nation seriously, and its need to justify its honor and independence, rather than any specific British act."

On June 18, 1812, Congress declared war on the United Kingdom, though without a single Federalist ballot. That same week, the British government, recognizing the damage inflicted by the American embargo, had rescinded the Orders of Council, but by the time that news slowly made its way across the Atlantic, muskets were being fired in anger. "Often criticized for vacillation, the president," the historian Jeff Broadwater has contended, "could have avoided an unnecessary war if only he had dithered a little longer." It should be noted, however, that though Federalists, conspicuously in New England, characterized the conflict as a Republican misadventure, doughty John Adams said that a "more necessary war was never undertaken. It is necessary against England; necessary to convince France that we are something: and above all necessary to convince ourselves, that we are not, Nothing." To have avoided war, Madison observed, "would have struck us from the high rank where the virtuous struggles of our fathers had placed us." The Presidential adviser Richard Rush, with an even longer sense of the reach of the past, declared that America was "the first genuine democracy engaged in a war since the ancients." He asked, "Shall we not reenact the splendid valor of Athens, of Thebes, of Rome?"

Presidents and Congress bear joint responsibility for taking the young nation into a war for which it was abominably unprepared after years of gutting defenses, though Madison had sought to persuade Congress to create an army of 20,000 and to call up 100,000 militiamen only to have Congress ignore his overture until the very last moment. In sum, the historian Robert Rutland has observed, "the

United States army was spread over a thousand-mile frontier, the navy was tiny enough not to crowd a single shipyard." Without the frigates the Republicans had refused to build, Adams warned Jefferson, "our Union will be a brittle China Vase." The British possessed 245 frigates to the Americans' seven; they had 191 larger ships of the line carrying a multitude of guns, the United States none.

The British advantage widened after Wellington's victory over the French at Waterloo liberated their forces to put down the presumptuous Yankees. The redcoats had won the admiration of Europe for their bravery in silencing the cannons of Napoleon's divisions. The troops who crossed the ocean to North America, said one British midshipman, were "eager souls, panting for fame and opportunity to sustain the laurels they had gained in many a bloody field of Spain and Portugal." His Majesty's jaunty infantrymen, inspirited by buglers and drummers playing lustily the notes of Handel's *Judas Maccabeus*, sang out loudly, "See the conquering hero comes / Sound the trumpet, beat the drums." In contrast, the United States entered the conflict with a small contingent of poorly led green soldiers, yet harbored the illusion that it was powerful enough to bring the British to their knees, and, while doing so, seize Canada. Madison, in his role as commander in chief, did not improve American prospects. "Nature has cast him in too benevolent a mould," Clay said. "He is not fit for the rough and rude blasts which the conflicts of Nations generate." Similarly, Andrew Jackson remarked that Madison, "a great civilian," had the outlook of a philosopher who "could not dwell on blood and carnage with any composure." A sympathetic biographer, Gaillard Hunt, later concurred. "In truth he was not an inspiring figure to lead in war," wrote Hunt. "The hour had come but the man was wanting. Not a scholar in governments ancient and modern, not an unimpassioned writer of careful messages, but a robust leader to rally the people and unite them to fight was what the time needed, and what it did not find in Madison."

Jefferson had once said that seizing Canada would be a "mere matter of marching," but that expectation did not prove out. Madison ordered General William Hull to invade Canada by crossing over from Detroit, only to have the elderly general surrender Detroit and his entire army instead. (Richard Rush called Hull a "gasconading bully! . . . a horrid coward," a somewhat unfair judgment because Hull was hampered by quarreling subordinates and a feckless secretary of war. Hull had reason, too, to fear another Indian massacre of civilians.)

The president also ordered an assault at Niagara led by an American general with no experience whatsoever of warfare. It, too, ended disastrously, with the surrender of nearly a thousand US soldiers. (The general reported on his troops: "Many are without shoes; all clamorous for pay; many are sick.") He was handicapped when New York militiamen, saying that they were pledged to defend their state but not to invade a foreign land, refused to advance into Canada. The third prong of Madison's strategy—to capture weakly garrisoned Montreal—fell short when American generals became involved in petty quarrels. Madison has often been criticized for his poor appointments of generals and cabinet officers, and poor they often were, but with Revolutionary War commanders superannuated, he had few commanders upon whom he could rely. Never before, Jefferson said, had there been "so wretched a succession of generals."

※※

The behavior of the executive and legislative branches put the nation's capital itself at risk. While spouting militant rhetoric, congressmen had so severely slashed funds for the army that money to defend Washington had to come from local banks. Madison, for his part, did not do enough to see to it that the city was stoutly defended, though he did alert his cabinet to the strong possibility that the British might very well choose to target the capital. Foolhardy aplomb persisted until the last moment. Madison's incompetent secretary of war dismissed reports of an approaching British incursion as "palpably a fable," and even the president, though more wary, told James Monroe, "This must be a great exaggeration." (Monroe wound up serving both as secretary of state and as secretary of war.)

That very day, the redcoats, having sailed up Chesapeake Bay, made landfall in Maryland. Ill-served by his subordinates, Madison, accompanied by Monroe, who had been assigned a role as commander, rode out to rally troops and consult with the maladroit US general. The American forces, the president informed his wife, "are in high spirits," and, according to the information he had received, the British "are not very strong . . . and of course . . . are not in a condition to strike . . . Washington." On the following day, at Bladensburg on the outskirts of the capital, in what may have been the worst performance ever by American men in arms, militiamen outnumbering the British nearly 2–1 panicked, unnerved by screeching incendiary Congreve rockets, and fled in pell-mell retreat without discharging a musket.

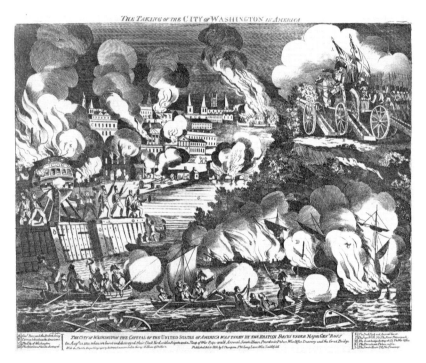

During the 1814 attack on Washington, viewed here from the Potomac River, the British forces razed most of the edifices of the US government. They drew international condemnation for setting fire to the President's House. When they completed their devastation, Washington was a city of embers. A large number of leaders favored abandoning the site altogether and moving the capital inland. *Library of Congress, LC-DIG-ppmsca-31113*

A letter from Dolley Madison to her sister Lucy provides the most vivid account of what ensued:

Tuesday Augt. 23d. 1814.

Dear Sister

. . . I have pressed as many cabinet papers into trunks as to fill one carriage. . . . I am determined not to go myself, until I see Mr. Madison safe, and he can accompany me, as I hear of much hostility toward him, . . . disaffection stalks around us. . . . My friends and acquaintances are all gone. Even Col. C. with his hundred men, who were stationed as a guard in the enclosure.

Wednesday morng., twelve o'clock. Since sunrise I have been turning my spyglass in every direction and watching with unwearied anxiety, hoping to discern the approach of my dear husband and his friends; but, alas, I can descry only groups of military wandering in all directions as if there was a lack of arms, or of spirit to fight for their own firesides!

Three O'clock. . . . I am still here within sound of the cannon! Mr. Madison comes not; may God protect him! Two messengers covered with dust come to bid me fly; but I wait for him. . . . Our kind friend, Mr. Carroll, has come to hasten my departure, and is in a very bad humor with me because I insist on waiting until the large picture of Gen. Washington is secured, and it requires to be unscrewed from the wall. This process was found too tedious for these perilous moments; I have ordered the frame to be broken and the canvass taken out . . . and the precious portrait [one of several copies by Gilbert Stuart] placed in the hands of two gentlemen of New York for safe keeping. And now, dear sister, I must leave this house or the retreating army will make me a prisoner in it, by filling up the road I am directed to take. When I shall again write to you, or where I shall be tomorrow, I cannot tell!

(Dolley Madison's missive is so compelling that historians find it irresistible, but some doubts have been raised about the accuracy of her account.)

With so few caring enough to impede their way, the British swept into Washington like a Visigoth horde. At the White House (not yet its official name), Admiral George Cockburn of the Royal Navy, who had been ravaging coastal towns and had set Havre de Grace ablaze, helped himself to the president's wine and raised a mocking toast: "Jemmy's health." He then ordered the White House burned to the ground—the hand-carved gilded chairs, the golden damask curtains, the bedding, the magnificent pianoforte all devasted. "The Cossacks spared Paris," observed the *London Statesman*, but we spared not the capitol of America." The arson, the British claimed, was in retaliation for the Americans' demolition of a Canadian capital—York, modern-day Toronto. (The deplorable burning of York, US officials maintained, was not calculated American policy but the work of rogue Yankee troops agitated by an explosion that killed General Zebulon Pike. Furthermore, the British had already achieved revenge by devastating Buffalo and other border American communities.) It should be noted that the British general in Washington had gone out of his way to assign a Scottish officer to protect the property of American homeowners along Pennsylvania Avenue.

The redcoats also torched most of the other government buildings. A senator's wife, deploring the demolition of the House of Representatives, reported: "Those beautiful pillars . . . were crack'd and broken, the roof, that noble dome, painted and carved with such beauty and skill, lay in ashes beneath the smouldering ruins." They set fire, too, to thousands of books in the Library of Congress. At the office of the *National Intelligencer*, Cockburn, called by Napoleon "rough, overbearing, vain, choleric, and capricious," ordered his marines to smash the presses and "destroy all C's so they can't abuse my name."

Their mission accomplished, the British departed the city and headed for Baltimore where, by the rockets' red glare, they would find a different reception. Expecting that his Majesty's fleet would level Baltimore's principal redoubt, Fort McHenry, they anticipated that the port would be compelled to pay tribute. But the city's forces, led by a Revolutionary War veteran, fought bravely. (One of those in the ranks was the seventy-one-year-old grandfather of Edgar Allan Poe.) On a boat in the harbor that night, a lawyer, Francis Scott Key, assigned by President Madison to rescue a doctor held by the British, was in the thick of the fighting and witnessed the bombs bursting in air. Fort McHenry flew a huge American flag, and when the doctor

Cockburn in the Chair.

It is said that Sir George Cockburn, a British Royal Navy officer, leaped into the Speaker's chair as his followers filled the halls of Congress and shouted, "Shall this harbor of Yankee democracy be burned? All for it will say Aye!" Before arriving in North America, Admiral Cockburn had gained a nasty reputation as a vindictive conqueror, and in the War of 1812, he advocated destroying all of the US capital city. Subsequently, the British government rewarded him with appointment as Knight Commander of the Order of the Bath and assigned him to convey Napoleon to exile on the island of Saint Helena. *The Miriam and Ira D. Wallach Division of Art, Prints and Photographs: Picture Collection, The New York Public Library*

asked if the flag was still there, Key, by the dawn's early light, could assure him that it was. The sight of the stars and stripes, not the Union Jack, signaled that the fort had withstood the British assault. Key then jotted down a poem about their experience, which, set to music, was adopted as the US national anthem, "The Star-Spangled Banner."

(Soundly repelled, the British fled to Halifax or their West Indian possessions.)

As soon as he heard that the enemy had cleared out, Madison, whose flight on horseback to Virginia had denied the enemy the opportunity to march him in manacles through the streets of London, galloped to Washington. He found a disheartening wasteland of soot and cinders. "He looks miserably shattered and woe-begone," an associate noted. "In short, . . . heart-broken." Federal officials were unnerved; the town's residents were seething. Graffiti read, "George Washington founded this city after a seven years' war with England—James Madison lost it after a two years' war." (Many of the fulminations against Madison were unfair. A man with no previous military experience, he had exercised command by dismissing inept commanders and replacing them with able generals, among them Winfield Scott and Andrew Jackson. He had also put James Monroe in charge of defense of the city of Washington. When citizens of the capital proposed to surrender to the redcoats, following the example of Alexandria, which had turned over all its ships plus numerous other valuables, Monroe, instructed by the president, told them that any delegation that approached the enemy would be "repelled by the bayonet." Madison, who spent countless hours in the saddle, also rode bravely to the battlefield.) Some members of Congress wanted to move the capital to someplace such as Lancaster or abandon it altogether. The president, with a newfound commitment to leadership, would not hear of it.

Madison established quarters in the Octagon House, a few blocks from the White House; arranged for Congress to occupy the Post Office and Patent building; ordered his cabinet to reassemble; and summoned Congress into special session. Determined that the White House be rebuilt as a replica of the burnt structure, he called back James Hoban, who, along with Benjamin Henry Latrobe, resurrected the original design and added two porticoes. Above all, President Madison had the good sense to realize that in a time of crisis the head of state must be a visible presence. As he made his rounds astride his dapple gray, he instilled confidence in the continuity of the republic.

When he delivered a message to Congress, he dismissed the British assault as an episode that "had interrupted for a moment only the ordinary public business of the Seat of Government."

Despite his valiant efforts, however, some Americans could not be rallied. Though Madison won re-election in 1812, opposition to the war was so fierce, especially in New England, that he barely survived. "To my ears," said a New England senator, Timothy Pickering, "there is no magic in the sound of Union. If the great objects of union are utterly abandoned—much more if they are wantonly, corruptly, and treacherously sacrificed by the Southern and Western States—let the Union be severed." The *Connecticut Courant* asserted that the war "was commenced in folly, . . . proposed to be carried on with madness, and (unless speedily terminated) will end in ruin." Instead of contributing to a national effort, New Englanders chose to concentrate their thin resources on local defenses, especially after the British devastated Connecticut ports such as Pettipaug Point (latter-day Essex). The Connecticut governor would not even respond to a US commander's call for militia to fortify New London and New Haven. At a convention in Hartford, it appeared that opponents of "Mr. Madison's War" might carry their hostility to the point of New England's secession from the union. When the gathering adjourned without going that far, a patrician, Harrison Gray Otis, found a morsel of satisfaction in the thought "that the little Pigmy shook in his shoes at our approach."

As the fighting ground on, both sides expressed an interest in peace and agreed to enter into negotiations in the city of Ghent (in modern-day Belgium), but they did so with markedly different attitudes. The Americans sought surcease; the British believed they could win the war and enjoy the fruits of victory. They advanced a staggering series of demands, insisting that the United States cede almost all of Maine north of the Penobscot where numerous citizens, accepting what they assumed was a fait accompli, had been taking oaths to George III. The British also demanded that Americans bow to the creation of an Indian buffer territory that would cost the United States the area that later formed the states of Illinois, Wisconsin, and Minnesota, and deny

Midwestern states access to the Great Lakes on which only British warships would be permitted. They also insisted that the United States give up fishing rights in the North Atlantic. "Oh, may no false liberality, no mistaken lenity . . . interpose," urged London's *Times*. "Strike! Chastise the savages, for such they are! . . . With Madison . . . no treaty can be made. . . . Our demands may be couched in a single word—Submission!"

The staunch US delegation at Ghent, chaired by John Quincy Adams, refused to submit, and the British reconsidered. The American success in Baltimore and, even more, the repulse of the redcoats at Plattsburgh and on Lake Champlain led Whitehall to question its assumption of eventual success. When Prime Minister Lord Liverpool sought to place the Duke of Wellington in command of His Majesty's North American forces, Wellington responded that the British people would not tolerate further bloodshed, and if he were to cross the ocean, it would be "to sign a peace which might as well be signed now." The ensuing treaty of Ghent contained not one of Britain's humiliating demands, though it did provide for postwar arbitration of some issues. When Madison, expecting the worst, read the terms of the pact, he was jubilant, and the US Senate ratified it unanimously. Madison rejoiced that the republic had emerged from the war intact. Still, as the military historian Donald Hickey has commented, "The war of 1812 looked more to the past than to the future. As America's second and last war against Great Britain, it echoed the ideology and issues of the American Revolution. . . . In this sense, the War of 1812 was the last of the North American colonial wars."

＊-＊

The War of 1812 ignited a resurgence of nationalism, as Jefferson had foreseen. "The war," said Treasury secretary Albert Gallatin, "has renewed and reinstated the national feelings and character which the Revolution had given." Though in the treaty that ended the conflict in 1815 the British acknowledged none of the US grievances but merely agreed to restore the status quo ante bellum, Americans chose to believe that they had won a second war of independence. John Quincy Adams might fume that "it is so notorious that the issue of our late war . . . was at best a drawn game," only "the most egregious national vanity . . . can turn it to a triumph," but few heeded. On sending the Ghent treaty up to the Hill, Madison told the US Senate, "I congratulate you, and our constituents, upon an event which is highly honorable to the nation, and terminates, with peculiar felicity, a campaign signalized by the most brilliant successes." The historian Daniel Walker Howe has asserted that "if the war and its economic hardships had dragged on much longer, the federal government . . . might not have survived intact." With Madison yearning to expand the US military effort, he had been forced to confront the alternative reality that the country was fast approaching bankruptcy. Secretary Gallatin had even urged resort to stamp taxes, a recommendation that appalled members of Congress who had fought in the American Revolution. But when peace came, humiliating defeats such as Bladensburg were forgotten.

The country chose to remember instead glorious naval victories on Lake Erie, where Oliver Hazard Perry reported, "We have met the enemy and they are ours," and on Lake Champlain, where, Commodore Thomas Macdonough informed the president, "The Almighty has been pleased to grant us a signal victory." Americans admired, too, the exploits of USS *Constitution* ("Old Ironsides"), which got the better of HMS *Guerriere* off the coast of Nova Scotia and sank the British frigate *Java* in Brazilian waters. Commodore Stephen Decatur's *United States* not only vanquished a British frigate off the Madeira coast but lugged it all the way across the Atlantic to New London, Connecticut, as a prize of war. Midwesterners, in particular, rejoiced at the outcome of a battle at the Thames in Ontario that resulted in the death of the formidable Shawnee chief, Tecumseh. "Peace," the Richmond *Enquirer* declared, "finds us covered with glory, elevated in the scale of nations. . . . The sun never shone upon a people whose destinies promised to be grander."

Above all, Americans celebrated feisty Andrew Jackson's astounding triumph at New Orleans, which upset the gloomiest expectations of the damage that would be wrought by the powerful British armada. "If an attack has been made on Orleans," the *New-York Evening Post* had told its readers, "the city has fallen." George III's navy, it stated, had spent the Christmas holidays savoring its conquest. In reality, Jackson, having put together a tatterdemalion force of Tennessee volunteers, Mississippi dragoons, French-speaking Louisiana militia, Jean Laffite's pirates, free blacks (who were promised land grants Jackson never delivered), even slaves (whom Jackson later returned to their masters), backwoodsmen, Haitians, Choctaws, and an Irish-American regiment, inflicted heavy losses on the proud redcoats, commanded by the Duke of Wellington's brother-in-law, Sir Edward Pakenham, who died in the fighting. Americans suffered few casualties, the British more than two thousand. "The lopsided numbers," Madison's biographer Noah Feldman has written, "were like something out of medieval myth—an American Agincourt."

Many contemporaries attributed this tremendous feat to Jackson, "The Hero," remarking that it did not matter whether the triumph originated with the "consummate skill and genius of the American commander," or whether one considered him "a chosen instrument of Heaven." A congressman declared: "Had this man lived before Hesiod wrote and Homer [sang], temples would have risen to his honor; altars would have blazed—and he would have taken his stand with Hercules and Theseus, among the immortals." Jefferson congratulated Madison on "the éclat with which the war was closed." (Unbeknownst to either side—in an age of slow trans-Atlantic communication—the battle had been fought and men had died more than two weeks after the end of hostilities had been negotiated in Ghent.)

In the postwar era, the country began to flex its muscles. "The war," asserted Gallatin, "has renewed and reinstated the national feelings and characters which the Revolution had given." Supreme Court Justice Joseph Story stated, "Never did a country occupy more lofty ground: we have stood the contest, single-handed, against the conqueror of Europe; and we are at peace, with all our blushing victories thick crowding on us. If I do not much mistake, we shall attain to a very high character abroad."

In this new age, the United States boldly asserted it power. When the Barbary states resumed their piratical attacks on US vessels, Madison demanded that Congress declare war and dispatched naval squadrons. After blockading Algiers, Stephen Decatur threatened to destroy the port unless the dey (the ruler) liberated American sailors he had enslaved, ceased demanding protection money, and paid indemnity. When the dey balked, Madison fired off a warning: "The United States, whilst they wish for war with no nation, will buy peace with none. It is a principle incorporated into the settled policy of America, that as peace is better than war, war is better than tribute." Cowed, the dey backed down, as did the potentates of Tunis and Tripoli.

In this climate of nationalism, Madison jettisoned many of the tenets of Jeffersonianism. Congress obliged him by enacting the country's first protective tariff, a moderate departure. Congress also allocated $100,000 for a federal highway through Wheeling, a segment of an ambitious plan to build a National Road linking Baltimore at the Chesapeake Bay with St. Louis at the outlet of the Missouri River that coursed through the vast hinterland explored by Lewis and Clark. In addition, Madison remedied gaps in defenses when he secured funds to bolster coastal fortifications after his secretary of war, James Monroe, said, "By the war we have acquired a character and rank among other nations which we did not enjoy before. . . . We cannot go back." When in 1816 Congress chartered the Second Bank of the United States, John Randolph charged that Madison had "out-Hamiltoned Alexander Hamilton." (Indeed, the Second Bank was capitalized at $35 million in contrast to Hamilton's $10 million.) Noting that Republicans had emerged politically triumphant, the historian Garry Wills later asked, "But did Republican *policies* win?" He answered: "If opposition to centralization, federal power, and nationalism was crucial to their policies, then John Randolph had a point when he said that they won by losing their souls." While Republicans embraced the principles of the Federalists, some New England Federalists, notably at the Hartford Convention, had lauded states' rights. "Our two great parties," commented John Adams, "have crossed over the valley and taken possession of each other's mountain."

Yet the embrace of nationalism was not total, and the new Republican emphases owed less to Madison than to the determination in Congress of Henry Clay and his followers to foster an "American System" with a magnified role for the federal government. On his final day as president, Madison surprised the country by vetoing a bill sponsored by Clay for "internal improvements" (roads and canals) on the grounds that it exceeded the powers of Congress and, though an admirable conception, could be achieved only by a constitutional amendment. "No circumstance, not even an earthquake that should have swallowed up half this city, could have excited more surprise," Clay later commented. The veto served as a shot across the bow to warn that, though Madison and Jefferson had somewhat modified their views, the Constitution still imposed limits on federal power. Madison had earlier rejected Hamilton's broad reading of the general welfare clause, and he continued to object that such an interpretation would vest Congress with plenary power that the framers of the Constitution had denied it. A striking instance of assertion in a presidency earlier characterized by deference, the veto demonstrated that, however much the executive office grew in the early nineteenth century, the expansion did not necessarily imply aggrandizement of the presidency or of a Hegelian national state.

⇥⇤

When commentators, at the time and later, reflected on the course of the War of 1812, nothing impressed them more than Madison's restraint in not taking advantage of an opportunity for enlarging presidential power. With his encyclopedic knowledge of past pitfalls of governance, Madison had once articulated a warning to himself:

> In war, a physical force is to be created, and it is the executive will, which is to direct it. In war, the public treasures are to be unlocked, and it is the executive hand which is to dispense them. In war, the honours

and emoluments of office are to be multiplied; and it is the executive patronage under which they are to be enjoyed. It is in war, finally, that laurels are to be gathered, and it is the executive brow they are to encircle. The strongest passions, and most dangerous weaknesses of the human breast; ambition, vanity, the honorable or venial love of fame, are all in conspiracy against the desire and duty of peace.

With keen memories of the debates in Philadelphia in 1787, Madison, in his conduct of the war, repeatedly showed his respect for the principle of separation of powers and for the Bill of Rights. "Although few Presidents have been subjected to so much personal invective and abuse," the historian Drew McCoy has written, "he never hinted at measures abridging freedom of speech or press, even in face of rampant obstruction of his government's policies and countless cases of outright treason." Madison had been called upon to fend off a mighty world power and had been required to cope with disruptive elements at home, a contemporary commentator pointed out, "without one trial for treason, or even one prosecution for libel." More than a century later, Garry Wills went so far as to maintain that, with regard to civil liberties in wartime, James Madison's record "is much better than that of Abraham Lincoln or Woodrow Wilson or Franklin Roosevelt."

The president's comportment sweetened the postwar polity even, to an astonishing degree, in New England, which had been so hostile to him and his war. Participants in a mass gathering in Boston sent him an apology for the wartime behavior of their region and praised him for "defending our commercial rights from foreign Aggressions, & maintaining the honor of this American Flag against those who had arrogantly assumed the Sovereignty of the Ocean." Bay State Republicans expressed confidence that grateful citizens "will commemorate your Name in the American Annals with lasting honor & Applause."

During his last months in office, Madison became what he had never been before: a popular president. "He was, after all, one of a dwindling band of surviving Revolutionary leaders," the historian

Jack Rakove has observed, "and that alone commanded the respect of younger generations of Americans." Despite "a thousand Faults and blunders," John Adams said, Madison had "acquired more glory and established more Union than all his three Predecessors, Washington, Adams, Jefferson, put together."

In his final address to Congress, Madison, surveying the state of the nation, told citizens how well they had performed in the war and how splendidly they were doing in its aftermath, the country enjoying piping prosperity. He knew that his own tobacco, which had sold for 3 cents a pound in 1812, had skyrocketed to 14 cents in 1816. Exports of flour to Liverpool soared from 19,000 barrels in 1816 to more than 538,000 barrels in 1817. Henry Adams, in his ambitious history of these times, asserted, "Every serious difficulty which seemed alarming to the people of the Union in 1800 had been removed or had sunk from notice in 1816. With the disappearance of every immediate peril, foreign or domestic, society could devote all its energies, intellectual and physical, to its favorite objects. . . . The continent lay before them, like an uncovered ore-bed."

Madison declared: "These contemplations, sweetening the remnant of my days, will animate my prayers for the happiness of my be-loved country, and a perpetuity of the Institutions under which it is enjoyed." And in the election of 1816, he found affirmation when the nation, by a whopping margin, chose to send one of his cabinet officers, James Monroe, to the White House as his successor. When Madison departed Washington by steamboat, a fellow passenger re-ported that the retiring president "was as playful as a child, talked and jested with every body on board, & reminded me of a school boy on a long vacation."

Some two centuries later, scholars differ clamorously in their assess-ments of Madison in office. "His presidency," Fred Greenstein declared, "is widely viewed as the undistinguished anticlimax to an exception-ally distinguished career," and Garry Wills has portrayed Madison as a man "who planned the government brilliantly but was lackluster in conducting it." Madison, Wills added, was a "hapless commander in chief." Other historians, though, reach a more positive conclusion, which will very likely prevail. "Madison's character, as well as his republican vision, took form in the enlightened, neoclassical age of the American Revolution," Drew McCoy has observed, "and his reflections during the retirement years reveal his persistent effort to comprehend—and to influence—the fate of that Revolutionary vision." Noah Feldman has carried the commendation still farther by asserting that "although Washington and Jefferson are more famous, the United States is Madisonian much more than it is Washingtonian or Jeffersonian," for Madison had "designed our most fundamental political structures and our most lasting categories of political thought." That judgment reveals that any evaluation of Madison's impact on the institution of the presidency will never rest solely on his performance in the White House but will rely, too, on his role as father of the Constitution, contributor to *The Federalist*, sponsor of the Bill of Rights, and creator of the first political party, which, it has been pointed out, is "still flourishing as the world's oldest political party."

6

James Monroe

Enunciating a Doctrine for the Ages

To demonstrate that Jeffersonian republicanism had survived the trial by fire of the War of 1812, Madison could not have had a more appropriate successor than his secretary of state. To a fault, James Monroe had demonstrated that he was a true believer in the Republican creed. As envoy to France in the 1790s, he had revealed himself to be even more Francophile than Jefferson—to such a degree that President Washington ordered his recall. When Monroe arrived back in America, Jefferson was at the harbor to greet him. A generation after eighteenth-century dress had gone out of style, Monroe still wore proudly the swallow-tail coat, the powdered wig (gray hair in a queue tied in back by a black ribbon), the tricorne hat, the blue coat, the ruffled shirt, the buff knee breeches with silver buckles, the black silk hose, and the white-topped boots of Patriots in the era of the War for Independence.

The nation could not know that Monroe would be the final member of the Virginia Dynasty, but it did treasure him as one of the last of the American Revolution pantheon. At seventeen, he had taken part in an assault on the governor's palace in Williamsburg, and a year later, as a recruit in the Third Virginia Infantry, he had given a good account of himself in General Washington's struggle to save Manhattan from the redcoats. At eighteen, Lieutenant Jim Monroe had volunteered to cross the Delaware in an advance unit for Washington's daring

Christmas night foray against the Hessians in Trenton, where he was badly wounded in a perilous charge. Only impromptu surgery saved him from bleeding to death. As president, Monroe carried a shoulder wound from the musket ball that had pierced him. He had also shown his mettle during the brutal Valley Forge winter, and, after Lafayette was shot at Brandywine Creek, Monroe, nineteen years old, gained his lifelong gratitude by caring for the marquis. "Monroe, for the rest of his life," observed his biographer Harry Ammon, "worked to convert the ideals of the Revolution ... which would serve as a model ... to the rest of the world." Jefferson gave him a letter of introduction to Madison that said: "The scrupulousness of his honor will make you safe in the most confidential communications. A better man cannot be." Jefferson said of Monroe: "Turn his soul wrong side outwards and there is not a speck on it."

Not all of Monroe's contemporaries held him in such high regard, though for the most part they thought well of him. A political pamphleteer asserted, "His best friends allow him to be but of moderate capacity, and slow of comprehension," and a former New York governor called Monroe "slow, passionate and dull." William Wirt, writing in *The Letters of the British Spy*, said of Monroe: "Nature has given him a mind neither rapid nor rich; and therefore, he cannot shine on a subject which is entirely new to him." Still, "to compensate him for this he is endowed with a spirit of generous and restless emulation, a judgment solid, strong and clear, and a habit of application, which no difficulties can shake, no labours can tire." In like manner, John C. Calhoun concluded about Monroe: "Tho' not brilliant, few men were his equals in wisdom, firmness and devotion to the country. He had a wonderful intellectual patience; and could above all men that I ever knew, when called on to decide an important point, hold the subject immovably fixed under his attention until he had mastered it in all of its relations. It was mainly to this admirable quality that he owed his highly accurate judgment. I have known many much more rapid in reaching a conclusion, but few with a certainty so unerring."

The federal city Madison turned over to Monroe in 1817 bore numerous grim reminders of the British arson three years earlier. The inauguration ceremony could not take place in the Capitol because it had been devastated, and when the House and Senate squabbled about an appropriate venue, the rite was moved outdoors for the first time. Despite the impromptu arrangements, Monroe was sworn in (by Chief Justice Marshall) before the largest crowd ever to assemble for the event. Some spectators had come from places as distant as New York via a novel form of transportation: the steamboat.

Six months elapsed before the Monroes could occupy the executive mansion, for the nation's capital remained a swampy outpost with only pretensions to grandeur. "We want nothing here," said impudent Gouverneur Morris, "but houses, cellars, kitchens, well-informed men, amiable women, and other little trifles of the kind, to make our city perfect." On New Year's Day 1818, the presidential couple hosted the first public reception in the renovated building with the highlight of the scene the restored portrait of George Washington. Since the exterior of the mansion had been daubed white even before the British charred it, people had taken to calling the home by an informal name: the White House. (Not until Theodore Roosevelt's administration would that designation become official.) With exquisite taste, the Monroes ordered Louis XVI furniture, including lengthy *canapés* (formal sofas), an ornate chandelier, tapestries, caryatids, ormolu clocks (no nudes), and marble mantels from France. Generations later, presidents continued to dine off their fine china (porcelain ware decorated by eagles carrying olive branches). "Most guests were likely to describe the president as plain and unassuming," the historian Noble Cunningham has commented, "but they depicted the White House as elegant, splendidly furnished, even magnificent."

Just as the Federalists had been criticized for aping British monarchical customs, the Monroes were chided for mimicking the pretensions of Parisian salons, but the presidential family dismissed the fault finders. First Lady Elizabeth Monroe, it was noised about, even painted her face in the manner of French ladies of fashion. Undeterred,

During his first term, James Monroe ordered the first china ever created for a US president from a firm in Paris. At the center of each plate an eagle carries a red, white, and blue banner declaring "E Pluribus Unum." The border contains designs representing agriculture, strength, commerce, science, and the arts. The president and First Lady Elizabeth Monroe brought heightened elegance to the White House. For years afterward, their French imports would embellish presidential soirees. *University of Mary Washington, The James Monroe Museum*

President Monroe, though his political sensibility was Doric, shared the conviction of his Federalist predecessors that the young republic needed *panache*. He knew that his wife, "La Belle Américaine," whose beauty had turned heads in Paris, was an asset. A Scandinavian envoy reported that "at the first court" she wore "a white gown of India mull, embroidered with gold, her hair . . . braided with pearls and adorned with a lovely diadem of gold set with pearls." After one White House gala, an observer said that she was "certainly the finest looking woman I saw," seeming scarcely older than her daughter.

James Monroe governed in high style. No longer, as with Jefferson, did European diplomats come upon a disheveled American head of state, and he dressed US diplomats in blue coats embroidered in gold or silver and lined with silk. Crimson satin brightened gilt chairs. The city of Washington liked to think that it took on some of the cosmopolitan elegance of a world capital. One American commentator even claimed that it had attained a "splendor which is really astonishing." In sum, the historian George Herring has written, "As much as Jefferson's style had symbolized the republican simplicity of an earlier era, Monroe's marked the rise of the United States to new wealth and power."

⋆⋆

Monroe also fostered a spirit of national unity far removed from the Federalist-Republican acrimony of 1800. "Never," the president had announced in his inaugural address, "did a government commence under auspices so favorable, nor ever was success so complete." He maintained, "Discord does not belong to our system." In his first year in office, he made a triumphal tour of the Northeast that spotlighted the emergence of an epoch of one-party or no-party politics. Wherever he stopped, he was regarded not as a partisan but as head of state. In Trenton, one of the scenes of his heroism in the Revolutionary War, hundreds of veterans lined up to salute him and grasp his hand as they called out to the man who had been a Patriot officer: "Brandywine, Sir!" "Monmouth, Sir!" His attire in "the revolutionary fashion," said the New Haven *Herald*, brought to mind the times that had "'tried men's souls.'" Monroe "made himself personally known, thereby touching new generations with something of the glamor of the revolutionary age," the historian Stuart Gerry Brown has stated. "They had seen and heard one of the Founding Fathers."

In Boston, so recently a hub of dissension against Mr. Madison's War, forty thousand admirers cheered Madison's chosen successor. At Bunker Hill, Monroe supervised a review of militia. On the fourth of July, thousands of schoolchildren greeted him on Boston

Common—girls in white, boys in Patriot blue coats and buff trousers. Each carried a rose: red or white to symbolize the melding of political parties. Longtime Federalists fell over themselves to pledge fealty to a Republican icon. Engaging in what Abigail Adams called ceremonies of "expiation," Federalists sought to expunge the opprobrium of disloyalty and "get back into the great family of the union," as Monroe said later. "During the late Presidential Jubilee," a Federalist editor reported, "many persons have met at festive boards, in pleasant converse, whom party politics had long severed." He gave an enduring name to the period by headlining an account of Monroe's journey ERA OF GOOD FEELINGS.

Monroe carried his mission of reconciliation through much of New England and then as far west as Detroit. He demonstrated that, like Washington, he understood that one requirement of this novel institution of a presidency was to enact political theater. In Vermont, he paid heed to the nurse who had dressed his wound at Trenton. In Kennebunk, in the District of Maine, Monroe stated that "we possess . . . a community, not only of interest, but of sympathy and affection," and in New London, Connecticut, the mayor celebrated a time "when party spirit is assuaged, and a spirit of mutual charity . . . nationally prevails." The first president to visit the West, Monroe was the first to be able to assure constituents in Ohio who had ventured across the Alleghenies that the government at the distant Potomac bore them in mind. Subsequently, he toured the frontier states of Kentucky and Tennessee on a demanding five-thousand-mile expedition. Near the end of his presidency, Monroe said that he had sought "to consolidate the people of the Union towards one another and to mitigate the asperities of party spirit."

For a long while, historians have contended that "Era of Good Feelings" is a misnomer for the Monroe years, but the rubric does convey Monroe's aims for his presidency. In his 1817 annual message to Congress, he rejoiced that "at no period of our political existence had we so much cause to felicitate ourselves at the prosperous and happy condition of our country." At the time of the address,

The slogan "Era of Good Feelings" is exemplified in this painting by John Lewis Krimmel of the 1819 Independence Day festivities in Philadelphia's Centre Square. People of all ages and classes joyously celebrate a Glorious Fourth during the presidency of James Monroe. One participant plays a fiddle while at his feet a dog forages. Above the tent on the left waves the Stars and Stripes of a united nation, below which appears a portrait of George Washington above a banner depicting a naval victory in the War of 1812 with the rallying cry "Don't give up the Ship". *Alamy*

he had already revealed that a desire to sustain national unity had been the driving force in his construction of a cabinet. From New England, to be secretary of state, he plucked John Quincy Adams, son of the former Federalist president. The Middle States maintained representation when he kept on as attorney general Richard Rush of Pennsylvania. Monroe also made a feint toward the West by offering the post of secretary of war to a Kentuckian, but when that ploy failed, he awarded the position to John C. Calhoun of South Carolina, giving a decidedly Southern cast to his administration. "Era of Good Feelings" served Monroe ill politically, though. Without a rival party to target, he had scant leverage with Congress, and the Republican Party fractured into factions.

Fully three decades after the founding convention in Philadelphia, Monroe presided over a minimalist state. The entire executive department numbered only 165 employees. The whole workforce of the State Department, including a watchman, totaled fourteen. Determined to reduce the cost of government, Congress, at a time when America was menaced by foreign foes, not only slashed appropriations for coastal fortifications, but reduced the US army to a mere six thousand officers and men. When Monroe toured the country on official business, he was required to meet expenses out of his own pocket. Congress did not provide money for even one secretary for the president, who had to lean on his family for clerical chores. Deprived of staff, Monroe was constantly occupied. Samuel F. B. Morse, commissioned by the city of Charleston to paint a portrait of the president, complained, after setting up an easel in the White House, "He cannot sit more than ten or twenty minutes at a time." John Quincy Adams, bemoaning the "multiplicity of business always crowded upon the President," ascribed the difficulty to Monroe's "want of an efficient private secretary."

James Monroe maintained the conception of a reticent presidency and a constricted national government. "The president," the biographer Fred Kaplan has written, "thought and acted deliberately; . . . preferred delay to action, prudence to spontaneity . . . with a commitment to the predominance of Congress and a narrow construction of the Constitution." When the Panic of 1819, the republic's first major depression, wracked the country, causing severe rural hardship and urban joblessness, the president, while acknowledging that "an unvaried prosperity is not to be seen in every interest of this great community," found "much to rejoice in the felicity of our situation." He refrained from federal intervention to cope with the travail, save to ease credit requirements for buyers of Western lands. The losses people sustained, he sermonized, were valuable as "mild and instructive admonitions" to the American people to restore republican virtues of "simplicity and purity." John Quincy Adams noted, "On the pecuniary embarrassments of the country, the distressed and decayed state of manufactures, . . . little was said," adding, "I think the message will be found meagre by the public." Attention centered on Congress, not the White House. "The Executive has no longer a commanding influence," observed US Supreme Court Justice Story. "The House of Representatives has absorbed all the popular feeling and all the effective power of the country."

><

In February 1819, Congress revealed Monroe's vulnerability when it began discussion of the request of Missouri territory to be admitted into the union as a state. That appeared to be a routine matter of the sort that had been taken up many times in the first generation of the republic, but it became incendiary when a New York representative, James Tallmadge Jr. of Poughkeepsie, sponsored an amendment in the House barring additional slavery in the slave state of Missouri and mandating gradual emancipation.

Response to the Tallmadge amendment shook the country. The ensuing controversy, said Missouri's territorial delegate, "produced a greater sensation in Congress than was almost ever witnessed before," and the former head of the Continental Congress found that the Missouri dispute "seems to have run like a flaming fire thro our middle states." Especially dismaying was the prospect that the "empire of liberty" Jefferson had created in the Louisiana Purchase would, with Missouri the first state (save for Louisiana) carved out of it, herald a vast domain for the expansion of slavery that would disfigure the United States ever after. One of Tallmadge's New York colleagues in the House, speaking of settlement west of the Mississippi, asserted, "Our votes this day will determine whether the high destiny of this region, and of these generations, shall be fulfilled, or whether we shall defeat them by permitting slavery, with all its baleful consequences, to inherit the land." A New Hampshire congressman declared:

> An opportunity is now presented, if not to diminish, at least to prevent, the growth of a sin which sits heavy on the soul of every one of us. By embracing this opportunity, we may retrieve the national character, and in some degree, our own. But if we suffer it to pass unimproved, let us … be consistent, and declare that our Constitution was made to impose slavery, and not to establish liberty. Let us no longer tell idle tales about the gradual abolition of slavery.

In contrast, Southern slaveholders, horrified by the attempt to restrict Missouri, threatened secession. "Men talk of a dissolution of the Union with perfect nonchalance and indifference," reported Virginia's John Tyler. The demand that Missouri be compelled to eliminate slavery "had kindled a fire … which seas of blood can only extinguish," said a Georgian member of the House. "If a dissolution of the Union must take place, let it be so!" Tallmadge riposted, "If civil war, which gentlemen so much threaten, must come, I can only say, let it come! … If blood is necessary to extinguish any fire which I have assisted to kindle, I can assure gentlemen, while I regret the necessity, I shall not forbear to contribute my mite."

Moderates feared that the barely suppressed discord over slavery might explode, but Clay forged an agreement in which the admission of Missouri would be balanced by that of Maine (hitherto a part of Massachusetts) as a free state and a line was drawn across the Louisiana Territory demarcating a southern area open to slavery and a considerably larger northern region closed to it. The controversy, which legislators thought had been resolved by their compromise, flared up again when Missouri adopted a constitution not only blocking emancipation but forbidding "free negroes and mulattoes from coming to and settling in this State"—a flagrant denial of a citizen's privileges and immunities that anticipated the vile Dred Scott opinion of the US Supreme Court in response to a later racist action in Missouri. Clay, though, once more eased the country out of this showdown by a formula that, as the historian Robert Pierce Forbes has written, was "deliberately obfuscatory."

Far from being a passive observer of these developments, as he sometimes has been presented, Monroe acted decisively. Though he was prepared to veto any legislation that incorporated the Tallmadge amendment, he collaborated out of sight with the Senate majority leader to bring about the Missouri Compromise. "I have never known a question so menacing to the tranquility and even the continuance of our Union as the present one," he said. He anticipated that "this question will be winked away by a compromise," and when one emerged from Clay's pen, he supported it by actions such as enlisting the Philadelphia banker Nicholas Biddle to herd Pennsylvania legislators behind it. When the Virginia junto tongue-lashed Monroe, a slave owner, for consenting to restrict slavery expansion, saying they "would not yield the 19th part of a hair," he held his ground.

Although it staved off a confrontation, the Missouri Compromise left considerable unease. Jefferson commented: "This momentous question, like a firebell in the night, awakened and filled me with terror. I considered it at once as the knell of the Union. It is hushed, indeed, for the moment. But this is a reprieve only, not a final sentence." Jefferson's oft-quoted words were once viewed as a denunciation of slavery. In fact, he blamed the threat to the union on Northern agitators who he suspected, unreasonably, were covert Federalists seeking a return to power by attempting to impose authority over slavery that the Constitution did not provide. And since no one had figured out a plan to compensate owners for loss of their property of costly slaves and to expel Blacks from the South, "we have the wolf by the ear, and we can neither hold him, nor safely let him go." If the federal government were to violate states' rights by abolishing slavery, he said, "all the whites within the United States south of the Potomac and Ohio must evacuate their States, and most fortunate those who can do it first." Jefferson concluded: "I regret that I am now to die in the belief that the useless sacrifice of themselves by the generation of '76 to acquire self-government and happiness to their country is to be thrown away by the unwise and unworthy passions of their sons, and that my only consolation is to be that I live not to weep over it." They were engaged, he said, in an "act of suicide on themselves and of treason against the hopes of the world."

From a diametrically different perspective, John Quincy Adams set down in his diary: "I take it for granted that the present question is a mere preamble—a title-page to a great, tragic volume." Adams also foresaw that "if slavery be the destined word of the destroying angel which is to sever the ties of this Union, the same sword will cut . . . the bonds of slavery itself. . . . It seems to me that its result might be the extirpation of slavery from this whole continent, and, calamitous and desolating as this course of events . . . must be, so glorious would be its final issue that, as God shall judge me, I dare not say that it is not to be desired."

Monroe deplored bondage as an "outrage upon the goodness of God," and he sought to cooperate with the British, led by their foreign secretary Stratford Canning, in suppressing the slave trade (an effort sabotaged by foes in the Senate), but, like Jefferson, Monroe saw no possibility that emancipation could lead to a biracial society. He looked forward to the day when "free blacks, who lived by pilfering," and "corrupted slaves" were no longer in the United States. Finding a racially integrated society inconceivable, he favored instead the removal of freedmen to West Africa. Toward that end, he helped the American Colonization Society acquire land holdings in Africa and authorized the US navy to transport Black settlers to the land that came to be called Liberia. Appreciation of the president emerged in the name for the capital of the new country: Monrovia.

The president's desire to achieve sectional harmony via the Missouri Compromise reflected a quest for reconciliation that was the dominant theme of his tenure, but the disappearance of partisan bickering had the unfortunate consequence that when Monroe ran for re-election in 1820 with no opposition, popular interest in national politics had receded to the point that less than 1 percent of eligible voters troubled to go to the polls. There was little to bring them out, for the dwindling corps of Federalists could not survive the accusations of treason hurled at them during the Hartford Convention, and no other faction challenged the Republican monopoly.

Monroe could take satisfaction in the 1820 outcome, however. In the 1816 campaign, he had made just one statement about his nomination for the presidency: "I can only say that, should the suffrages of my fellow-citizens call me to that trust, I should feel a duty to enter on it." In 1820, he had no need to utter a word. That year, Monroe received every electoral vote but one. (It has traditionally been said that William Plumer of New Hampshire gave his ballot to John Quincy Adams so that George Washington alone would have the distinction of being a unanimous choice. In fact, Plumer, a Federalist, did not care for Monroe and thought Adams an abler man. In his diary, Adams, on learning of Plumer's action, recorded his "mortification.") Still, for Monroe the results were not only a personal victory but proof that he had achieved his goal of national unity. Monroe's triumph, though, did not enhance his power. "Mr. Monroe has just been re-elected with apparent unanimity," commented Henry Clay, but he had "not the slightest influence on Congress. His career was considered as closed. There was nothing further to be expected by him or from him."

In his second term, as at times in his first, Monroe uttered eloquent, occasionally fussy, avowals of adherence to constitutional restraints. Like Madison, he insisted that a constitutional amendment was required before Congress could appropriate money for internal improvements, and he vetoed a bill for collection of tolls on the Cumberland Road—America's national turnpike, moving west from Cumberland, Maryland, for 620 miles. On the question of whether

Congress could derive the power to promote growth of the infrastructure from the text of the Constitution, Monroe expressed his "settled conviction . . . that Congress do not possess the right. It is not contained in any of the specified powers granted to Congress, nor can I consider it incidental to or a necessary means."

Yet while singing from the hymn book of respect for the Constitution and limited powers, Monroe moved the country well beyond Jeffersonian parameters. Aware that Montesquieu, in *De L'Esprit des Loix*, had contended that republics could not survive in a large territory, Monroe insisted that by creating a federal network of roads and canals "we shall shorten distances and . . . shall bind the Union more closely together." Though continuing to believe that the national government must not invade local spheres, he signed bills that gave money to states to repair the Cumberland Road, to survey routes linking the Ohio Valley and Lake Erie, and to enable Treasury investment in the Chesapeake and Delaware Canal Company.

Monroe also favored other nationalist programs. He made a point of turning up at the first exhibition of products manufactured in the United States, a show staged in the rotunda of the Capitol, and in 1824 he signed legislation imposing a protective tariff. In addition, he sounded more than a little like Alexander Hamilton in stating that a national bank would "attach the commercial part of the community in a much greater degree to the government, . . . the great desideratum of our system." Under Postmaster General Return J. Meigs II, the United States enormously expanded the number of post offices and post roads essential for linking the back country to the more populous seaboard. Finally, Monroe obtained federal funds to finance an expedition by Major Stephen Long of the Corps of Topographical Engineers to explore by steamboat the vast Missouri basin and other western river valleys. The expedition was the high point of Monroe's nationalist inclination, the outlook of a president who more than any of his predecessors felt at home in the burgeoning West.

❊

In foreign affairs Monroe made his biggest mark, largely because he wisely heeded the counsel of John Quincy Adams, all but universally regarded as America's greatest secretary of state. No one has ever come to that position with more impressive credentials. As a twelve-year-old, Adams had dined with Jefferson in Paris; at fourteen, fluent in French, he had been secretary of the US legation in St. Petersburg; and, while only twenty-seven, he had held the post of minister to The Hague. Subsequently, he had served as the first envoy plenipotentiary to the Kingdom of Prussia, where he translated Christoph Martin Wieland's romance, *Oberon*, and warned of Napoleon, "the Corsican ruffian." George Washington had called him "the most valuable character we have abroad." As his country's first minister to Russia, he became a favorite walking companion of Tsar Alexander I. At Ghent, he had been the chief US commissioner charged with persuading the British to terminate the War of 1812 without requiring cession of American territory, and he went on to be appointed minister plenipotentiary to Great Britain. He also served as Boylston Professor of Rhetoric and Oratory at Harvard.

As the prolonged rupture with Great Britain swiftly healed after the peace of Ghent, the Monroe administration succeeded in defining America's northern border with British North America (later Canada). The Rush-Bagot pact of 1817 reduced the permissible size of each country's fleets to no more than a token force on the Great Lakes and Lake Champlain, a settlement called by the diplomatic historian Samuel Flagg Bemis "the first reciprocal naval disarmament in the history of international relations." (Not a treaty but an executive agreement, the pact left the strict constructionist Monroe so squeamish that he asked the US Senate to determine whether "this is such an arrangement as the Executive is competent to enter into, by the powers vested in it by the Constitution, or is such an one as requires the advice and consent of the Senate.") Adams achieved a second accord with the British, the Convention of 1818, which set the country's northern border from the Lake of the Woods to the Rockies at the 49th parallel and provided for joint American-British occupation of Oregon through the ensuing decade, renewable there-after. In return for America's dropping its demand for the right to fish anywhere in Canadian waters, Britain also guaranteed the former colonials access to fishing grounds to dry and cure their catches off Newfoundland and Labrador "for ever." (Furthermore, an 1824 pact fixed the southern limit of Russia's holding in Alaska.)

Like his Republican forerunners, Monroe combined belief in limited government with lust for territory, and the most precious prize was the Spanish possession of Florida. His concentration on Florida, though, derived from more than a desire to extend the US domain to the Gulf of Mexico. With the disintegrating Spanish em-pire unable to exercise control over its land across the sea, Florida became a safe harbor for Seminole Indians and brigands assaulting pioneer families in the Southern states. Amelia Island off the Atlantic coast of Florida sheltered pirates. (So, too, did Galveston in Mexico, which provided a base for the scary Jean Lafitte.)

Not many months after he took office, Monroe sent General Andrew Jackson into Florida in pursuit of Indian marauders. The president knew that he was courting trouble because on the very day that he was inaugurated Jackson had informed him that he had instructed officers to disobey any order from the administration that did not first go to the general, and Monroe had found it necessary to rebuke him. Jackson further revealed his attitude by telling the secre-tary of war, "I have the pleasure to inform you that I am now at the head of 2,070 volunteers . . . who have no constitutional scruples." Monroe, though, may well have reckoned that, while leaving him-self deniability, he could count on the reckless Jackson to behave in a manner that would persuade Madrid that it could no longer hold on to Florida. No one doubted Jackson's fortitude. He showed so much toughness on his march south from Tennessee that his soldiers called him "Old Hickory."

In short order, Jackson demolished Seminole communities, arrested the Spanish governor, seized Spanish ports, invaded the fortified post of St. Mark's, where he hauled down the Spanish flag, hanged two

Seminole chiefs, and created an international incident by executing two British subjects, one of them the Scot Alexander Arbuthnot, an idealist with a humane concern for the fate of Indians. "I am informed that you have orders to fire on my troops entering the city," Jackson asserted in a belligerent note to the Spanish commander in Pensacola. "I wish you to understand distinctly that if such orders are carried into effect, I will put to death every man found in arms."

Outraged, the Spanish government demanded that Jackson be punished, a course echoed by most of the cabinet and by leaders in the US Congress. Henry Clay urged his colleagues in the House to remember that "Greece had her Alexander, Rome her Caesar, England her Cromwell, France her Bonaparte." If Jackson were not censured, the failure to do so would be "a triumph over the constitution." Monroe, while returning two of the forts to Spain, refused to discipline Jackson for exceeding his authority, though he did scold him, and even confided that the general's "attack may produce a good effect in promoting a cession" by Spain.

The border troubles ultimately found resolution when, under the Adams-Onis pact of 1819, the United States acquired all of Florida, though not before Monroe considered arbitrarily occupying the area. The pact also assigned the United States the claims of Spain in Oregon. The acquisition cost no more than $5 million, paid not to Madrid but to Americans with claims against Spain. Adams, a brilliant negotiator, secured recognition of favorable western boundaries of Florida. In this agreement, which bore the name of Transcontinental Treaty, he persuaded the Spanish to acknowledge a demarcation that ran all the way to the Pacific Ocean. "The Florida Treaty," John Quincy Adams wrote in his final years, "was the most important incident in my life, and the most successful negotiation ever consummated by the government of this Union." Sustaining that judgment, Samuel Flagg Bemis subsequently characterized the agreement as "the greatest diplomatic victory won by any single individual in the history of the United States."

In 1822, taking advantage of the power presidents had assumed to recognize new regimes, Monroe asked Congress to appropriate funds for diplomatic missions to five republics that had broken away from Spain: Chile, Colombia, La Plata (modern-day Argentina), Mexico, and Peru. The United States, Monroe declared, was setting an example in becoming the first country to grant recognition to these former dependencies in the "cause of liberty and humanity." The rest of the world was unimpressed. France threatened to restore Spanish rule, and the tsar indicated he might intervene. To warn them off, British Foreign Secretary Canning approached the US minister in London with a proposition: a joint Anglo-American admonition. "What do you think your Government would say to going hand in hand with England?" he asked.

That question prodded Monroe to an action that, though by a serpentine path, secured his place in history. He was initially inclined to fall in with the British proposal, an extraordinary overture from a recent enemy that both Jefferson and Madison endorsed, but he developed second thoughts. Secretary Adams countered, as he noted in his diary, that "it would be more candid, as well as more dignified, to avow our principles explicitly to Russia and France than to come in as a cockboat in the wake of the British man-of-war." Adams also insisted that Monroe accompany a statement of hemispheric solidarity with an avowal of self-denial. In particular, he warned Monroe off recognizing Greek independence from Turkey. "The ground that I wish to take," Adams said, "is that of earnest remonstrance against the interference of the European powers with South America, but to disclaim all interference on our part with Europe." Adams outlined a set of principles that could be enunciated in diplomatic communiqués. Monroe agreed, but he chose to express these thoughts with dramatic flair in his annual message to Congress in December 1823, announced from the rostrum of the House of Representatives with the president adorned in the academic garb of a robed professor.

In that document, much of it framed by Secretary Adams, though unmistakably the president's creation, Monroe sent European powers a blunt message: Hands off! The United States, he announced, would regard "any attempt" by European countries "to extend their system to any portion of this Hemisphere as dangerous to our peace and safety." In words aimed at discouraging Russian designs on the west coast of North America, he proclaimed that "the American continents . . . are henceforth not to be considered as subjects for future colonization by any European power." Placing these demands in the context of a distinction between Old World and New World political systems, he gave assurance that in "wars of the European powers, in matters pertaining to themselves, we have never taken any part, nor does it comport with our policy so to do." (He especially discouraged any effort to aid Greek rebels who had been calling for help from "fellow-citizens of Penn, of Washington, and of Franklin." He did so in part because he thought that such action would jeopardize trade relations with Turkey, though Clay objected that the refusal of the United States to rally to the cause of liberty meant that it was selling its soul for a "miserable invoice of figs and opium.") Monroe also stated that "with the existing Colonies or dependencies of any European power we have not interfered and shall not interfere." The president's primary emphasis was that "we could not view any interposition . . . by any European power" to oppress the new Latin American republics "in any other light than as the manifestation of an unfriendly disposition toward the United States." The composition had no legal standing, and not for many years would it be labeled the Monroe Doctrine. But from the first, Americans applauded Monroe's bold assertions, and in generations to come they would revere this presidential initiative in foreign policy, undertaken without consultation with the US Senate, as holy writ.

⟶⟵

By 1824, as Monroe's eight years in office were drawing to a close, the near-unanimity of 1820 had fractured. No longer was it possible for the Virginia Dynasty to impose an orderly succession. New York's Martin Van Buren, who did more than anyone to create what would become known as the Democratic Party, tried to preserve the old ways by summoning a Congressional caucus that could be counted

Thomas Sully's 1829 portrait of James Monroe in retirement suggests his serenity as he reflects upon a job well done but also his perturbation about what the future might hold. When he died two years later, the divisive Andrew Jackson was roiling the nation, and no one any longer spoke of living in an era of good feelings. The hanging of this portrait in the diplomatic reception rooms at the US Department of State suggests the enduring significance of the Monroe Doctrine. *Funds donated by Mrs. Thomas Lyle Williams, Jr., in memory of her husband, The Diplomatic Reception Rooms, U.S. Department of State, Washington, DC, RR-1967.0049*

on to nominate Monroe's secretary of the treasury, William Crawford of Georgia, but, to the cry of "King Caucus is dead," more than two-thirds of the members of Congress boycotted the meeting. Hezekiah Niles, one of the country's most prominent editors, said of the traditional method, "I would rather that the halls of Congress were converted into common brothels than that caucuses . . . be held in them."

The contest for the nomination, which with no viable Federalist candidate meant election to the presidency, vexed Monroe. Three of the aspirants were in his cabinet, and he expressed "embarrassment" at their vying for preferment. Furthermore, a number of the rivals chose to gain advantage by attacking Monroe's policies as departures from Jeffersonian orthodoxy. Crawford, in particular, undercut Monroe by misrepresenting the condition of government finances and by pressing for retrenchment. Van Buren, on behalf of Crawford, even denounced "Monroe heresy." At one point, Monroe, believing that Crawford was going to assault him, picked up fire tongs to defend himself. A more formidable candidate than Crawford was Andrew Jackson, who was portrayed as the virtuous champion of common folks, for he was "never in *Europe*" and "never the HEAD OF A DEPARTMENT."

The president passed up the opportunity to follow Jefferson and Madison in designating a member of the cabinet as his successor. As secretary of state, John Quincy Adams held the historically favored position for succession to the presidency, but the stiff-necked Yankee said that if the White House entailed "cabal and intrigue," he sought "no ticket in that lottery." He also announced, "I make no bargains. I listen to no overtures for coalition." He did, though, want the office, even to the point of hosting a ball in honor of Jackson's triumph at New Orleans that drew a thousand guests to his F Street home to drink punch and honor the Hero. One critic accused him of parroting Shakespeare's Macbeth, who had said, "If chance will have me king, why chance may crown me, without my stir."

In the ensuing national election, Andrew Jackson, publicized as legatee of the values of the American Revolution, finished first, with 99 electoral votes, trailed by Adams (84), Crawford (41), and Clay (37).

Jackson, it has been reckoned, got 41 percent of the popular vote, followed by Adams with 32 percent, Clay with 13 percent, and Crawford with 11 percent. (These are traditional estimates. Some recent research has allocated more popular votes to Adams, pushing him ahead of Jackson in that tally, but not altering the electoral count, which was all that mattered. Jackson's advantage in the Electoral College, it should be noted, derived from the three-fifths provision of the constitution that, by giving three-fifths of the voting allocation to slaves, though they were deprived of suffrage rights, overstated his strength below the Mason-Dixon Line. Without that provision, Jackson would have received 77 electoral votes, fewer than those recorded for Adams.)

Since none of the four had won a majority in the Electoral College, the contest moved to the House of Representatives, which had to choose among the top three vote-getters. That stipulation of the Twelfth Amendment eliminated Clay, who had fewer electoral votes though more popular votes than Crawford, resulting in his being cast in the position of kingmaker. A dashing figure who had fought more than one duel and was a silver-tongued orator, "Gallant Harry of the West" had a fervent following beyond the Alleghenies. Abraham Lincoln called him "my beau ideal of a statesman, the man for whom I fought all my humble life." In accounting for how Lincoln came to identify with a particular political party, Dennis Hanks said his cousin Abe "always loved Hen Clays Speaches I think was the Cause Mostly."

Clay took advantage of his enormous popularity to determine the outcome of the 1824 contest. If John Quincy Adams were designated, Clay reasoned, that outcome would not "inflict any wound upon the character of our institutions, but I should much fear . . . that the election of the General would give the military spirit a stimulus . . . that might lead to the most pernicious result." Acutely aware of the fragility of the republic that had been created, the first generation of leaders walked in fear of a Cromwell. Van Buren later recalled that a prominent Virginia editor "scarcely ever went to bed without apprehension that he would awake to hear of some *coup d'etat* by the General." Similarly, Daniel Webster recorded Jefferson's sentiments: "I feel much alarmed at the prospect of seeing General Jackson President. He is one of the most unfit men I know for such a place. . . . His passions are terrible. When I was President of the Senate, he was a Senator; and he could never speak on account of the rashness of his feelings. I have seen him attempt it repeatedly, and as often choke with rage. His passions are no doubt cooler now . . . but he is a dangerous man."

On a snowy February day in 1825, Clay played the decisive role in persuading a preponderance of state delegations in the House to elect Adams president of the United States. At a time when democracy was on the march, Adams, at Clay's behest, got Kentucky's backing, though the New Englander had not won a single vote in that state and though the Kentucky legislature had instructed Clay to support Jackson. (The final outcome, however, was not wholly the result of Clay's maneuvers, for in states such as New York other figures pulled strings. In addition, Adams was not above activity on his own behalf, notably by bowing to the demand of Missouri's lone Congressman, who controlled his state's vote, that particular individuals be granted printing contracts.) The contest ended melodramatically when Clay announced from his speaker's seat at the head of the chamber: "John Quincy Adams, having a majority of the votes of these United States, is duly elected President of the same."

A number of considerations impelled Clay to favor Adams. Crawford had suffered a stroke that had initially left him speechless, nearly blind, and, in his own word, "deranged." Jackson, merely a "military chieftain," Clay dismissed by writing, "I cannot believe that killing two thousand five hundred Englishmen at N. Orleans qualifies for the various, difficult and complicated duties of the Chief Magistracy." Clay, in fact, held the Hero in contempt. He later told Sam Houston that Jackson was "certainly the basest, meanest scoundrel that ever disgraced the image of his God." Furthermore, nursing his own future presidential ambitions, Clay was disinclined to foster those of his only serious rival for the affections of Western voters. Not least, Adams's nationalistic program resonated with Clay's American System (an extensive infrastructure, tariffs, and a national bank) fostered by an interventionist federal government. Yet Clay did not commit himself until he had held a long conference with Adams, and he may have made his choice only after he had exacted something in return, albeit perhaps nothing coarsely explicit.

Jackson's supporters had no doubt that there had been a "corrupt bargain," especially after Adams appeared to anoint Clay as his successor by naming him secretary of state. Clay's acceptance of this appointment "was the worst political mistake the Kentuckian ever made," the historian Harry Watson has written. "All the waters of the sweet Heavens cannot remove the iota of corruption," said a Jacksonian congressman. The erratic John Randolph denounced this "stinking" conspiracy between the "puritan and the blackleg," likening Adams and Clay to Blifil and Black George, nefarious characters in Henry Fielding's *Tom Jones*. A Tennessee congressman reported: "The House was a perfect scene of confusion for half an hour, no one addressing the Chair, the Chairman crying out Order, Order, Order, hurley burley, helter skelter, Negro states and Yankee. Yes, says he—Mr. R.—with uplifted hands, I swear to my God and Country that I will war with this administration made up of the Puritans and Blacklegs." Adams wore "Puritan" as a badge of pride, but Clay challenged Randolph to a duel and fired a bullet through the Virginian's cloak. Jackson, in turn, resigned his Senate seat and, raging at Clay, returned home to prepare for revenge in 1828. "So you see," he said of Clay, "the *Judas* of the West has closed the contract and will receive the thirty pieces of silver. His end will be the same."

❖❖

Assessment of the Monroe presidency begins with the recognition that though James Monroe was scrupulously respectful of the curbs on executive powers mandated by the Constitution, he nonetheless made a considerable impress on the institution of the American presidency. John Quincy Adams even maintained that the Monroe administration would "hereafter . . . be looked back to as the golden age of this republic." In an epitaph composed for Monroe, Adams concluded that the last of the Revolutionary age soldiers in the White House "was entitled to say, like Augustus Caesar of his imperial city, that he had found her built of brick and left her constructed of marble."

Monroe had taken a number of bold steps. He authorized an executive agreement in foreign affairs and in 1822 became the first president to issue a signing statement when he put his signature on a bill reducing the size of the army, but declared that only he had the authority to appoint military officers. He also took advantage of what Theodore Roosevelt was to call the "bully pulpit" of his office to craft a sermon announcing the Monroe Doctrine. He had signaled how far-reaching his imperial ambitions were by sending two warships to Oregon coastal waters after earlier dispatching a frigate to a Pacific island near the Antarctic that promised a rich harvest of seals. He informed Congress, too, that he had found it "necessary to maintain a naval force in the Pacific for the protection of the very important interests of our citizens engaged in commerce and the fisheries in that sea," a big leap that was, as Noble Cunningham has pointed out, the first step in "the establishment of the Pacific station—a permanent stationing of naval vessels off the Pacific coast." Under President Monroe, US territory or claims extended across the continent from the Atlantic to the Pacific. The republic was becoming an empire.

7

John Quincy Adams

Advocating Activist Government

John Quincy Adams took office with an acute sense of embarrassment. Never before, he pointed out to a Congressional committee headed by Daniel Webster, had anyone become president with only a minority of electoral votes. "Perhaps two-thirds of the whole people," he acknowledged, had been "adverse to the actual result." He wished, he said, that there could be a new election so that citizens would have another opportunity to make their will known. But he knew that the Constitution made no provision for a second canvass. "I shall therefore repair to the post assigned me . . . oppressed with the magnitude of the task before me," he stated. "Less possessed of your confidence in advance than any of my predecessors," he told the American people in his inaugural address, "I am deeply conscious of the prospect that I shall stand more and oftener in need of your indulgence."

Already at a disadvantage because of the manner of his election, Adams had the further handicap of being, as he said of himself, "a man of reserved, cold, austere, and forbidding manners" who was perceived as a "gloomy misanthrope" and "an unsocial savage." In St. Petersburg, commented a British observer, Adams had been "of all the men whom it was ever my lot to . . . waste civilities upon . . . the most . . . systemically repulsive. With a vinegar aspect, . . . he sat . . . like a bulldog among spaniels." In later years, Ralph Waldo Emerson wrote in his diary that Adams "must have sulphuric acid in his tea." The first man elected to

This daguerreotype by Philip Haas of the sixth president in his later years projects the grim visage of the Yankee puritan. It is historically significant as the earliest surviving photograph of a US president. Adams has a melancholy look, though he was widely hailed as an exceptional ex-president and could take pride in his recommendations as president in urging initiatives by the national government that are the precursors of those advanced by successors from Theodore Roosevelt to Joseph Biden. *Gift of I. N. Phelps Stokes, Edward S. Hawes, Alice Mary Hawes, and Marion Augusta Hawes, 1937, The Metropolitan Museum of Art*

the presidency ever to be photographed, the short, balding man looks out from his portrait sternly, querulously, sourly. Raised in a regimen of self-denial, he had a "disposition," remarked James Buchanan, "as perverse and mulish as that of his father." In a Phi Beta Kappa address when he was a Harvard undergraduate, John Quincy Adams had maintained that the basis for a good marriage was reason, not passion, and that the most important consideration in choosing a wife was not love but her money. When his sons did not do well at Harvard, he banned them from the Christmas hearth, remarking, "I would feel nothing but sorrow and shame in your presence." Adams, echoing his father, acknowledged, "I well know that I never was and never shall be what is commonly termed a popular man," adding, with respect to his character, "I have not the pliability to reform it."

Bone and marrow a Puritan, he closely herded his emotions as his parents had catechized him to do. "I never knew a Man of great talents much given to Laughter," his mother told him. "You come into Life with Advantages which will disgrace you if your success is mediocre," his father, when vice president of the United States, lectured him. "If you do not rise to the head not only of your Profession, but of your Country, it will be owing to your own *Laziness, Slovenliness* and *Obstinacy*." When as a boy he had braved the Atlantic to accompany his father on an overseas mission, his mother, Abigail, had written him afterward, "Dear as you are to me, I had much rather you should have found your Grave in the ocean . . . or an untimely death crop you in your Infant years, rather than see you an immoral profligate or a Graceless child." She further instructed him, scarily: "Keep a strict guard upon yourself, or the odious monster will soon loose its terror by becoming familiar to you."

Ever mindful of her admonishments, the solemn lad, aged seven, wrote his father, "I hope I grow a better Boy and that you will have no occasion to be ashamed of me." Three years later, he reflected: "My Thoughts are running after birds eggs play and trifles, till I get vexed with my Self. Mamma has a troublesome task to keep me Steady, and I own I am ashamed of myself." Never was he left in doubt as to what

his mother expected of him: "Let your ambition be engaged to become eminent." The young man heeded. At nineteen, he entered in
his diary Shakespeare's lines: "If it be a sin to covet Honour / I am the
most offending soul alive."

Resolved to be a righteous statesman, Adams had entered the political arena contemptuous of the claims of party. As US senator from
Massachusetts, he had antagonized both Federalists and Republicans.
"Indeed," Joseph Ellis has written, "a conspicuous flair for alienating
voters while acting in their long-term interest, much like premature baldness, was bred into the genes of all prominent male members of the Adams line." At a time when New Englanders sought to
safeguard their profitable commerce with Great Britain, he was the
lone Federalist in Congress to vote for Jefferson's embargo. On more
than one occasion, he had even taken part in Republican gatherings,
which, his mother informed him, "staggered" her. Adams responded,
"I could wish to please my parents—but my duty I *must* do." Incensed
by his behavior, Massachusetts Federalists had ended his tenure in the
US Senate. Adams's admirers esteemed his principled comportment,
but his attitude handicapped him as president when called upon to vie
for public favor in the political arena in an era when party creation
was resuming.

≫⋅≪

In his very first annual message to Congress, on December 6, 1825,
Adams demonstrated his talent for annoying colleagues by presenting
a magisterial state paper that was extraordinarily imaginative but
stunningly impolitic. At a time of distrust of governmental power,
he proposed creating a vast network of roads and canals, a national
university, a naval academy to match the military institution already
founded at West Point, a uniform system of weights and measures,
and a Department of the Interior that would foster exploration in
places as distant as the shores of the Pacific. Noting that Europe had
more than one hundred "light-houses of the skies," he called upon
Congress to erect the country's first astronomical observatory to study

"the phenomena of the heavens." Adams also urged it to profit from the example of the British and the French who had been undertaking "profound, laborious and expensive researches into the figure of the earth and the comparative length of the pendulum vibrating seconds in various latitudes from the equator to the pole." He had a gargantuan ambition that he later articulated: "the ultimate improvement and exaltation of the nature of man and his condition on earth."

Members of Congress found the new president's language even more shocking than his proposals. "While foreign nations less blessed with . . . freedom . . . than ourselves are advancing with gigantic strides in the career of public improvement, were we," he asked, "to slumber in indolence . . . and doom ourselves to perpetual inferiority?" It was "with no feeling of pride as an American," he added, in a period of Yankee brag, that notice need be taken of how far superior Europe was to the United States in scientific research. These remarks not only told Yankee doodle dandies that they were backward but also called attention to the years Adams had spent in foreign lands. Far worse was another adjuration. Lawmakers, he lectured them, should not "proclaim to the world that we are palsied by the will of our constituents." Those ill-chosen words, departing so radically from the Jeffersonian view that officials were to be guided by popular desires, came at an especially inappropriate time when politicians were increasingly intent on catering to the people. Jefferson himself saw the message as a revival of the Federalists with their younger members "having nothing in them of the feelings or principles of '76 . . . look[ing] to a single and splendid government of an Aristocracy" that would crush "the plundered ploughman and beggared yeomanry."

In contrast to the Jeffersonian perception that liberty is preserved by diminishing the national state, Adams boldly declared that "liberty is power." Unlike his predecessor James Monroe, who quailed at assertion of federal authority that lacked clear constitutional sanction, Adams in his inaugural address maintained that "unborn millions of our posterity" would express thanks for roads and waterways that should be created without delay. In this first State of the Union

address, he went still further by calling for "laws promoting the improvement of agriculture, commerce and manufactures, the cultiva-
tion and encouragement of the mechanic and of the elegant arts,
the advancement of literature, and the progress of the sciences, orna-
mental and profound." Failing to do so "for the benefit of the people,"
he scolded, "would be to hide in the earth the talent committed to
our charge—would be treachery to the most sacred of trusts."

Nothing illustrates better the acceptance of the Virginia Dynasty's
conception of limited government and a restrained presidency than
the response to Adams's message. To be sure, chroniclers have often
exaggerated the hostility in the country to Adams's recommendations,
since there was considerable popular support for public works, but
rival politicians, especially in Congress, wanted to retain control of
"pork," not lose it to an ambitious chief executive. Senator Martin
Van Buren of New York deplored "ultra-latitudinarian doctrines";
Thomas Jefferson deemed particular proposals unconstitutional; and
Andrew Jackson denounced the message as a recipe for "despotism."
A North Carolina senator, taking aim at Adams's feckless language
in his address, vowed that he would never be "palsied" save by the
Constitution and the will of his constituents. Furthermore, said another North Carolina legislator, "If Congress can make canals, they
can ... emancipate." Indeed, Robert Pierce Forbes has written, Adams
"was probably doomed from the start because of the unwavering an-
tagonism of slaveholders and their allies. . . . The black hole of slavery
drew everything near it within its gravitational field." To a multitude
of critics, Adams's farsighted recommendations, as the biographer
Fred Kaplan has stated, were "a vision too far." Adams's document was
more than a century ahead of its time in imagining that a president
could guide the nation toward a society in which the central government would have a directing role.

Even projects that might not have been expected to raise objections went nowhere. The War of 1812 had revealed that British captains, knowing more than Americans about navigating the US coast,
sailed into coves where American captains feared to venture lest they

run aground, but Congress refused to authorize a coastal survey.
(Hearkening to local enthusiasm, though, it did agree to look into
the needs of Baltimore, Charleston, and Savannah harbors. Moreover,
piers arose at sites from Ashtabula and Sandusky in Ohio to Saco and
Stonington in New England, as well as, farther south, in New Castle
and Mobile.) Adams's initiative in naming US representatives to what
became the first Pan American Conference, promoted by Simón
Bolívar, the Liberator, to meet in Panama foundered. Southerners,
in particular, could not abide the prospect that American delegates
would be conferring on a basis of equality with Blacks from Haiti,
a country born of a slave insurrection. For asserting his rightful authority as chief executive to accept the invitation, Adams protested, he
was abused by John Randolph in the coarse language "of Hogarth's
Gin Lane and Beer Alley." Partisans in the House delayed appropriations so long that the lone US envoy to reach Panama arrived after
the meeting had adjourned. The design of a naval academy received
Senate approval, though barely, but the House rejected as absurdly expensive the notion of hiring nine professors for the academy at a total
annual cost of seven thousand dollars. Congress had no intention of
creating a national university or standardizing weights and measures,
and "light-houses of the skies" elicited guffaws.

Adams's manifesto did not go wholly unanswered. The Cleveland
and Akron Canal expanded the reach of the city on the lake, and the
Louisville and Portland Canal enabled vessels to skirt the Falls of the
Ohio, expanding opportunities for Cincinnati as well as Louisville
and Pittsburgh. Dayton prospered after the digging of the Miami
Canal. When ground was broken for the Chesapeake and Ohio Canal,
President Adams won plaudits by shedding his coat and driving a
spade through a balky root. The National Road, which started in
Cumberland, Maryland, rolled westward from Wheeling, Virginia,
to Zanesville, Ohio, which it would reach shortly after his term
ended. After he left office, he was instrumental in the founding of
the Smithsonian Institution, funded by a generous Englishman whose
bequest of half a million dollars crossed the Atlantic to America in

In this 1829 watercolor by Thomas Ruckle, covered wagons on a busy thoroughfare in Maryland demonstrate that travelers benefitted from a government-sponsored internal improvement program that provided the most modern route from the east to Zanesville, Ohio. Eventually, the National Road invited Americans to explore the trans-Mississippi West, expediting the greatest folk movement of the age. President John Quincy Adams advocated road construction sponsored by the national government as a significant way to bind the young nation. *Courtesy of the Maryland Center for History and Culture*

gold coins, and in 1843 Adams laid the cornerstone for America's first lighthouse in the sky, an observatory on an Ohio hillside named Mount Adams. He took advantage of the occasion to expatiate upon the history of astronomy from Pythagoras to Copernicus to Newton. (His alma mater, Harvard, also erected an observatory, and even the federal government sponsored a modest one on naval grounds in Washington.)

In foreign affairs Adams expanded his vision and his initiatives. He never flagged in his promotion of free trade, and he did achieve treaties in European markets with the Hanseatic League, as well as Prussian, Austrian, and Scandinavian commercial allies, starting with Denmark. Adams also expanded his horizons. As secretary of state under Monroe, he had said that America "goes not abroad, in search of monsters to destroy," but, as president, he turned his thoughts to helping the Greeks in their conflict with the Turks. Determined to safeguard his prerogatives, he refused to admit "the Senate or House of Representatives to any share in the act of recognition" of foreign governments.

While he was in the White House, however, victories were sparse, especially after a devastating midterm election that, for the first time in history, gave the opposition control of both houses of Congress. According him little respect, Congress enacted a trade law in 1828 so festooned with concessions to parochial interests that it was called a "tariff of abominations." He fared no better in his role as national head of a federal system. When white land speculators violated treaty commitments to the Creek nation, he contemplated using force, but the governor of Georgia, accusing him of allying himself with "savages," defied him, and the president could not muster an effective resistance. "John Quincy Adams had glaring faults as a political leader in an increasingly democratic and materialistic republic," concluded the historian Edward Pessen, "but in view of the unyielding nature of his enemies, . . . it is doubtful that his administration would have been a success . . . no matter how admirable his political program or how consummate his political skills."

In this season of adversity, Adams pursued equanimity by physical exertion and by immersion in intellectual endeavors. "I rise from bed, dress myself, and sally forth from my door in darkness and solitude," he reported, "cheered by the 'song of triumph' of Chanticleer." He also became a legendary figure in the history of the presidency by stripping himself and plunging into the Potomac, then drying off on its banks.

His greatest solace came from reading, especially the Bible and the Roman classics. He read the Old Testament and the New in French or German as well as English, and regretted he could not do so in Hebrew. He perused the Bible rigorously, unable to accept doctrines such as the Immaculate Conception. To comprehend what happened in ancient times, he commented tartly, "I believe it best not to attempt consulting the Bible and Herodotus together." He thought "the narrative part of the Bible, . . . according to all the rules of human evidence, more . . . [unimaginable] than the metamorphoses of Ovid." He found the classics less troublesome. "To live without having a Cicero and a Tacitus at hand," he recorded, "seems to me as if it was a privation of my limbs." He read both in Latin, absorbing Horace in the original as well. He also permitted himself a peek at Lord Byron's naughty cantos in *Don Juan*, which he found "very licentious and very delightful." (Adams used Byron's structure as a model, too, in churning out his own epic—a labor of ninety stanzas in rhyme.) Furthermore, his research in the natural world proved so impressive that he was elected president of the American Academy of Arts and Sciences.

⋟⋞

In 1828, Adams confronted fierce opposition to his bid for a second term. A hostile editor said of Adams and his appointees, "We will turn them out as sure as there is a God in heaven. . . . By the Eternal, if they act as pure as the angels that stand at the right hand of the throne of God, we'll put them down." The president's opponents flocked to Andrew Jackson, acclaimed as the herald of a new democratic order. It did not matter that Jackson identified with the Nashville elite, that he had often behaved despotically, that he was the master of slaves, or that he was a provincial of inchoate views. "Indeed," his advocate Martin Van Buren acknowledged, "Genl. Jackson has been so little in public life that it will be not a little difficult to contrast his opinions on great questions with those of Mr. Adams." When doubt was raised about whether Jackson was committed to republican values, Van Buren told an associate "that the General was at an earlier period well-grounded in the principles of our party, and . . . we must trust to good fortune and to the effects of favorable associations for the removal of the rust . . . contracted . . . by a protracted non-user, and the prejudicial effects in that regard of his military life." Besides, "the General's personal popularity" could be used to political advantage. As one of the foremost historians of the period, Harry Watson, puts it pithily, "The General . . . wrapped his intentions in a toga of republican ambiguity."

Van Buren's reference to "our party" was a bit premature, but the rudiments of a reconstituted two-party system did develop during the Adams presidency. When the supporters of Jackson, Crawford, and Calhoun joined forces against Adams, the coalition, a Richmond editor wrote Van Buren, cemented an alliance between "Southern planters and plain republicans of the North"—the core of what soon would be known as the Democratic Party. In the 1828 campaign, these allies papered over differences by uniting in an appeal to the masses on behalf of Old Hickory. Instead of relying on traditional methods, they sought to rouse popular support for him by erecting hickory poles, reminiscent of the liberty standards of the struggle against George III, and wearing hats adorned with hickory leaves. Adams and Clay countered by organizing what came to be called National Republicans, forerunners of the Whigs. Party warfare, Van Buren maintained, would "rouse the sluggish to exertion, give increased energy to the most active intellect, excite a salutary vigilance over public functionaries, and prevent that apathy which has proved the ruin of Republics."

The rebirth of party competition undoubtedly advanced the democratic process, but its advent in 1828 was not an edifying sight. The 1828 campaign, the historian Robert Remini has written, "splattered more filth . . . upon more innocent people than any other in American history." Foes of the administration alleged that when John Quincy Adams was the US envoy in St. Petersburg he had pimped for Tsar Alexander by seeking "to make use of a beautiful girl to seduce the passions of the Emperor . . . and sway him to political purposes." Not to be outdone, opponents of the Hero of New Orleans asserted, "General Jackson's mother was a COMMON PROSTITUTE, brought to this country by the British soldiers! She afterward married a MULATTO MAN, with whom she had several children, of which number General Jackson IS ONE!!!" They also accused Andrew Jackson of murder and adultery and his beloved wife, Rachel, of sexual misconduct and bigamy. When she died a few weeks after the election, and was interred in a white gown she had chosen for the inaugural ball, Jackson, heartbroken and bitter, pinned the blame for her death directly on Adams. He never forgave him.

In this supersaturated atmosphere, a candidate needed finely tuned political antennae, and Adams had none. He told crowds who congregated to cheer him to go home and mind their business. As the former head of the American legation in Berlin, he was fluent in German, but he was appalled when, required to dedicate a canal in Pennsylvania, he was called upon "to show myself among the German farmers and speak to them in their own language." He would not even attend the fiftieth anniversary of the battle of Bunker Hill.

Adams had appointed three men to his cabinet who had opposed his election, and he refused to reward those who stood by him. "Men who had worked tirelessly for his election," Harry Watson has stated, "could barely get so much as a limp handshake from John Quincy Adams, much less a federal appointment or a printing contract." Distributing patronage, the president said, "would be repugnant to my very soul." When Clay urged him to dismiss custom house officials in Philadelphia and Charleston who were brazenly sabotaging his presidency, Adams agreed that "they are no doubt hostile to the Administration," but he would remove no officer "for merely preferring another candidate for the Presidency." He acknowledged that Postmaster General John McLean was engaged in "deep and treacherous duplicity" by working egregiously for Jackson, but because McLean had "improved the condition of the Post Office Department since he has been at its head, and is perhaps the most efficient officer that has ever been in that place," Adams refused to cashier him. (McLean went on undercutting Adams, and, as a reward, Jackson subsequently appointed him to the US Supreme Court.) A high-ranking Marylander wrote plaintively that "we never shrink from Enemies or abandon our friends, but we expect sometimes to be gratified in preference to our Enemies and the Enemies of our administration."

Admirably principled, Adams, in showing his allies that they had nothing to gain by sticking with him and his foes that they had nothing to fear from him, all but guaranteed that his presidency would have a very sparse record of legislative achievement and that his quest for another term was in peril. Remini concluded: "It is really impossible to think of any other president quite like John Quincy Adams. He seemed intent on destroying himself and his administration. By the same token it is difficult to think of a president with greater personal integrity."

In his campaign for the White House, John Quincy Adams found himself at a significant disadvantage when matched against Andrew Jackson, who had become a creature of myth. Jackson's followers, observed the intellectual historian John William Ward, featured Old Hickory "as a child of the forest" who possessed "untutored genius." Ward also noted that Adams's opponents contended that the victory at New Orleans demonstrated that Jackson was "divinely chosen and his entire life was . . . proof of the assumption. The fact that Jackson alone of all his family survived the Revolutionary War proved that 'the ways of Providence are dark and inscrutable.'" Eulogists also found it significant that "Jackson's mother, . . . for the cause of the Revolution, offered up her whole family except for her last born son upon the altar of her country."

Campaign propagandists, undeterred by the reality that Jackson's meager qualifications compared poorly with the brilliant diplomatic career of John Quincy Adams from an early age, labored to turn the contrast topsy-turvy. A Massachusetts commentator said of Jackson that he "had not the privilege of visiting *the courts of Europe at public expense* and . . . glittering in the beams of royal splendor. . . . He was not dandled into consequence by lying in the cradle of state." And since Jackson had been "inured from infancy to the storms and tempests of life, his mind was strengthened to fortitude and fashioned to wisdom."

From 1824 to 1828, the electorate tripled, and a substantial majority of these voters preferred Jackson to Adams. By 1828, there was almost universal white manhood suffrage, with all but two states (Delaware and South Carolina) providing for the choice of electors by the people, not by legislators. Jackson did not cause this expansion, but he had some effect in stimulating interest, and he certainly profited from it. That year, he received 56 percent of the popular vote, the highest proportion given any presidential candidate in a contested election in the nineteenth century, and an emphatic 178–83 electoral triumph. In free states, however, Jackson received only 50.3 percent of the popular vote. His deceptively large showing derived from the 72.6 percent he ran up in slave states. Much more to the point is the historian Daniel Walker Howe's conclusion: "After 1828, the classical ideal of nonpartisan leadership, which Adams and Monroe had shared with Washington, . . . was dead—killed in battle with Old Hickory as surely as General Pakenham." (In retaliation for Adams's resistance to the exploitation of Indians, Georgia left the president's name off the ballot, so no one in that state could vote for him.) The notion that Jackson's victory represented a volcanic expression of democratic will is a misconception.

Haggard and despondent, Adams surrendered the presidency at a low point. "The sun of my political life," he said, "sets in the deepest gloom." Granted, he did not believe there was anything he "ought to repent," reaping satisfaction in the prosperity of the country. But he knew that his principal ambition had been thwarted. In contrast to the Virginia Dynasty, which had sought to cabin executive power, Adams had a broad conception of his mission, but he was never able to fulfill it during his tenure. Adams's "administration," his biographer Paul Nagel concluded, "was a hapless failure and best forgotten, save for the personal anguish it cost him." Adams himself characterized his presidency as "the wreck." Compounding his difficulties, he learned that one of his young sons, an alcoholic, had impregnated a servant and another had toppled to his death off a boat, quite possibly a suicide. He identified with Cicero, for he and the Roman had been "deserted by all mankind, . . . expelled from power, and rendered miserable by the loss of a much-loved child." Disconsolate over "deep humiliations which are thickening about me," Adams, in his last days in office, could not get out of his head lyrics he had first heard at Versailles that had been sung by a minstrel to the imprisoned Richard the Lionheart:

O, Richard! O, mon Roi!
L'univers t'abandonne.

"The four most miserable years of my life," Adams later said, "were my four years in the presidency."

☙❧

In this miserable final presidential year, John Quincy Adams could not imagine that after stepping down in 1829, he would almost immediately begin one of the most admirable and admired periods of his illustrious career. He was a man of pride but not so proud that he would pass up the opportunity to move from his lofty perch in the White House to a seat in the lower house of Congress. In 1830, he consented to run in a Congressional race in the Plymouth district, an appropriate venue for the aged Puritan. When he won overwhelmingly, he said that his elevation to the presidency had not been "half so gratifying" to his soul. Every two years thereafter, Massachusetts voters re-elected him right down to his death in 1848, in one blowout by more than 80 percent of the ballots. Throughout that period, starting at the age of sixty-four, he occupied the same chair near the dais in the House chamber, present all day long, "an elderly, small, bald, somewhat fragile-looking legislator," Fred Kaplan has written, "who, when he rose to speak, transformed himself into a sharp-tongued, gesticulating dynamo of moral passion and legislative cunning."

Congressman Adams quickly made his mark by leaping to the defense of remonstrances by Northern anti-slavery agitators who inundated the House of Representatives with thousands upon thousands of petitions calling for ending bondage in the District of Columbia and other federal territory. To Adams's dismay, a Southern bloc imposed a gag rule, rigorously enforced by Speaker James K. Polk of Tennessee, consigning the petitions, unread, unacknowledged, to oblivion. Month in, month out, year in, year out, Adams demanded revocation of this gag rule.

Adams did not readily embrace his role of gadfly on this issue. In common with other Founders, he could not envision a colorblind society. He found no pleasure in Shakespeare's *Othello*, he said, for Desdemona's "passion for a black man" elicited "disgust." Furthermore, he stressed that he did not wish to incite "mutual hatred" in the nation and certainly did not seek to incite a bloody "servile insurrection."

But the gag rule, he affirmed, represented a flagrant denial of the right to petition guaranteed by the Constitution and sanctified by God. "Petition was prayer," he maintained. "It was the cry of the suffering for relief, of the oppressed for mercy." The New England poet John Greenleaf Whittier captured Adams's outlook in writing:

> No seal is on the Yankee's mouth,
> No fetter on the Yankee's press!

In a letter to his constituents, Adams wrote: "Would the freemen of Massachusetts, the descendants of the Pilgrims, allow themselves to be manacled? Children of Carver, and Bradford, and Winslow and Alden! The pen drops from my hand!"

Through numbers of sessions, Congress readopted the gag rule, and Adams refused to be silenced. "My conscience presses me on," he confided. "Let me but die upon the breach." In one parliamentary maneuver, he submitted petitions from women of New England because, since they did not have the right to vote, they fell outside the proscription of the gag rule. A zealous Virginian called Adams "the acutest, the astutest, the archest enemy of Southern slavery that ever existed." Death threats crowded his mailbox. One man wrote him, "I'm in Covington, Kentucky. I am leaving now, and am coming for you, and I will cut you down on the street." Former First Lady Louise Adams beseeched the Lord: "Dark Terror round my spirit cling. Protect us 'gainst the murderer's hand. . . . For blood! For blood they lust!" An infuriated Southerner shouted, "I demand that you shut the mouth of that old harlequin!" But John Quincy Adams would not be silenced, and increasing numbers of his Congressional colleagues found the words of "Old Man Eloquent" persuasive. On December 3, 1844, the indefatigable Adams secured one of his greatest triumphs when Congress expunged the gag rule. In his diary, he set down, "Blessed, forever blessed, be the name of God!"

Adams chalked up another conspicuous victory for human rights when he involved himself in the *Amistad* controversy. In 1839, slavers abducted dozens of Africans and transported them to the dreaded destination of Cuba for a life of exploitation in the sugarcane fields. In Cuba, after they were sold into slavery, they were taken aboard a two-masted schooner, the *Amistad*. The Africans, led by Cinqué, mutinied, murdered the captain, and ordered two Spanish slave owners on the ship to sail them east to their homeland. Instead, the slave proprietors headed the vessel north, where it was overtaken by a US naval brig and wound up in the harbor of New London, Connecticut. Spain demanded that the *Amistad* be returned to its owners and the Africans sent to Cuba for punishment. The American government, not wanting to offend Southern slave interests, sought to oblige.

But Northern abolitionists rushed to the defense of the Africans, who were at risk of execution, and asked Congressman Adams to take part. Though he had not argued a case for three decades, he agreed to appear before the US Supreme Court on behalf of Cinqué and his companions. He readily demonstrated that the men, not born slaves, were captives. Pointing to a framed document on the wall, he said, "The moment you come to the Declaration of Independence, that every man has a right to life and liberty as an inalienable right, this case is decided. I ask nothing more on behalf of these unfortunate men than this Declaration." That was poor law, for the Declaration has no place in American jurisprudence, but effective argumentation. "Extraordinary," Justice Joseph Story said. "Extraordinary for its power and its bitter sarcasm, and its dealing with topics far beyond the record and points of discussion." In an opinion written by Story, the US Supreme Court resolved to grant the Africans their freedom. "There does not seem to us," Story said for the 7–1 majority, "any ground for doubt that these negroes ought to be deemed free." If

Westville Jan 4th 1841

Dear Friend

In this letter *Amistad* captive Kinna implores John Quincy Adams for help. The first American presidents advocated fair treatment for people of color but did not deliver much. After his term ended, and he won election to Congress, though, Adams argued successfully in the US Supreme Court for the liberation of the *Amistad* mutineers. *Adams Family Papers, Massachusetts Historical Society* many historians give a failing grade to John Quincy Adams's presidency, they also agree that the man was one of the very greatest ex-presidents in American history.

On a valedictory tour from Erie to Pittsburgh in his final years, Adams, who had so often been thwarted as president, found himself a popular icon hailed by large crowds for, as the historian William Cooper has observed, "the septuagenarian was not only the literal son of a major Founding Father; he had also actually known and spoken with George Washington, Benjamin Franklin, Thomas Jefferson, James Madison, and James Monroe—Founders all." Cooper concluded, "When he departed the Executive Mansion, the nation of the Founders left with him."

⋙⋘

John Quincy Adams spent a lifetime dedicated to the Patriot cause. Seared in his memory was the battle of Bunker Hill to which his mother, Abigail, had taken him when he was a little boy. Years later, he recalled "the thundering cannon, which I heard, and the smoke of burning Charlestown, which I saw on the awful day." He remembered, too, "the tears of my mother and mingled with them my own" brought on by the death of the "dear friend of my father," Dr. Joseph Warren, on that field of valor. Not content to compel her son to view this bloody melee, she insisted, as he later said, that he "repeat daily, after the Lord's prayer, before rising from bed, the Ode of Collins on the patriot warriors who fell in the war to subdue the Jacobite rebellion of 1745."

These grim beginnings stiffened his resolve ever after. In his college commencement address, he stressed adherence to the kind of self-sacrifice that had distinguished the brave warriors of the American Revolution. When in the War of 1812 others quailed at British redcoats' incursions on the American seaboard, Adams was unflappable. The Patriots of '76, he said, had bequeathed an assignment: "to preserve, to cherish, to *improve* the inheritance which they have left us—won by their toils . . . saddened but fertilized by their blood." The current generation, he declared, must be "worthy sons of worthy sires."

He maintained the faith even when the next generation faltered. "Between 1824 and 1828," William Cooper has written, "the political world of the Founding Fathers, which Adams idealized and to which he paid fealty, underwent wrenching transformation. . . . The old political order that he cherished was in its death throes." Adams's trust in the future of the American venture, however, was undimmed. "I could take by the hand as a fellow-Citizen a man born on the Banks of the Red River or the Missouri, with just the same cordiality that I could at least half a million natives of Massachusetts," he told a fellow Yankee. And he affirmed, "The whole continent of North America appears to be destined by Divine Providence to be peopled by one *nation*."

In his final years, John Quincy Adams found himself called upon to speak whenever America mourned the passing of yet another member of the Patriots of '76. When he delivered a tribute to James Madison in 1836, Adams told the Boston gathering, "From the saddening thought that they are no more, we call for comfort upon the memory of what they were, and our hearts leap for joy, that they were our fathers." In a eulogy after John Quincy Adams's death, a senator noted, "His father seemed born to aid in the establishment of our government, and his mother was . . . co-laborer of such a patriot. The cradle hymns of the child were the songs of liberty." And the famed orator Edward Everett asserted that "it may be fairly traced to these early impressions that the character of John Quincy Adams exhibited through life so much of what is significantly called 'the spirit of seventy-six.'"

Although, wrote the British traveler Harriet Martineau in 1838, "the tone of disappointment against Mr. Adams may sometimes rise to something too like hatred, there is undoubtedly a deep reverence and affection for the man in the nation's heart; and any one may safely prophesy that his reputation, half a century after his death, will be of a very honourable kind." She added, "He fought a stout and noble battle in Congress last session in favour of discussion of the slavery question, and in defence of the right of petition upon it; on behalf of women as well as of men. While hunted, held at bay, almost torn to pieces by an outrageous majority . . . he preserved a boldness and coolness as amusing as they were admirable." A considerably better known British author set down a similar judgment. "An aged, gray-haired man," John Quincy Adams was, in the view of Charles Dickens, "a lasting honour to the land that gave him birth."

Admiration for John Quincy Adams, however, derived very little from his performance as chief executive but primarily from his career as a diplomat before entering the White House or as the intrepid crusader against the gag rule after ending the presidency. Adams himself wrote a Salem clergyman in 1837, "My life will end in disappointment of the good which I would have done, had I been permitted. . . . I fell and with me fell, I fear never to rise again, . . . the system of internal improvement by means of national energies."

But it did rise again, and John Quincy Adams may now be seen, much more credibly than Jackson, as the prophet of the expansive modern state of the Square Deal, the New Deal, the Fair Deal, the Great Society, and Bidenomics. Later generations repeatedly rediscovered Adams and found reason to celebrate him. The penetrating twenty-first-century political columnist E. J. Dionne called John Quincy Adams his "favorite unsung president" because of his prophetic vision of the national government as the agent for "the progressive improvement of the condition of the governed." And in 2019, a drama celebrating Adams found twenty-first-century pertinence in his adherence to principle. The *Washington Post* headlined its review: "John Quincy Adams is the anti-Trump in the new play 'JQA.'"

Epilogue

The moment of highest drama in the first decades of the American presidency came not when John Quincy Adams turned over the White House to Andrew Jackson, but on a summer day nearly three years earlier: July 4, 1826. In Quincy, Massachusetts, where John Adams lay dying, the repeated roar of cannon to celebrate the Glorious Fourth was overpowered only by midafternoon thunder claps—called "the artillery of Heaven." Told the date, Adams responded, "It is a great day. It is a *good* day." Before death came, he whispered, "Thomas Jefferson survives." He did not know that six hours earlier, as church bells pealed in the valley below his hilltop estate, Jefferson had slipped away, but not before asking, according to legend, "Is it the Fourth?" President John Quincy Adams thought it "a strange and very striking coincidence" that these two patriots who had collaborated on drafting the Declaration of Independence should both succumb on precisely the fiftieth anniversary of the charter. In seeing "visible and palpable marks of Divine favour," he expressed the sentiment of many that the second and third presidents of the republic had died "amid the hosannas and grateful benedictions of a numerous, happy, and joyful people."

In a commemorative tribute delivered at Faneuil Hall, Daniel Webster saw in the occurrence proof that "our country, and its benefactors, are objects of His care." Earlier, Webster said, the loss of these Founders could have resulted in "an immense void," but, at this moment of Jubilee, their goals had been achieved, and the new generation could rejoice that the republic was "ours to enjoy, ours to preserve, ours to transmit." Webster added, "The tears which flow, and the honors that are paid, when the Founders of the republic die, give hope that the republic itself may be immortal."

When the first presidents looked back on the course of events since the launching of the republic, they chortled. John Adams took pride in his own role in the success of the American Revolution. Thomas Jefferson, though sometimes dismayed by the pursuit of the dollar by the next generation, found comfort in the conviction that "even should the cloud of barbarism and despotism again obscure the science and liberties of Europe, this country remains to preserve and restore light and liberty." He rejoiced that the "flames kindled on the 4th of July 1776 have spread over too much of the globe to be extinguished by the feeble engines of despotism." Jefferson maintained, "We can no longer say there is nothing new under the sun for this whole chapter in the history of man is new." And he confided, "I steer my bark with Hope in the head, leaving Fear astern." The historian Harry Ammon has written that "most Americans in the 1820s regarded the American Revolution as a sacred moment in the distant past, when a gallery of greats had been privileged to see God face to face," an image borrowed from Ralph Waldo Emerson.

Historians in the modern era have echoed these perceptions. Joseph Ellis has contended that "the British philosopher and essayist Alfred North Whitehead was probably right to observe that there have been only two instances in the history of Western Civilization when the political leaders of an emerging nation behaved as well as anyone could reasonably expect. The first was Rome under Caesar Augustus and the second was America's revolutionary government."

The outlook of the Framers, however, found expression, too, in an earlier remark by John Adams, who said that he liked "the dreams of the future better than the history of the past." They did not want their heirs to be intimidated by the belief that they could never measure up to their forefathers. Benjamin Rush even said that "there is very little difference in that superstition which leads us to believe in what the world calls 'great men' and in that which leads us to believe in witches and conjurors." Jefferson once noting that "some men . . .

ascribe to the men of the preceding age a wisdom more than human," then commented, "I knew that age well. I belonged to it, and labored with it. It deserved well of its country. It was very like the present, but without the experience of the present, and forty years of experience in government is worth a century of book-reading." The Framers realized, too, that they had not only done nothing to eliminate the bane of slavery but had even incorporated the vile serfdom in the Constitution.

Still, members of the new generation knew full well how much they owed to the Founders for what they had been bequeathed, and numbers of historians have agreed. During the early republic, David Ramsay of South Carolina asserted that the American Revolution had "not only required, but created talents." Men of '76, he declared, had acted "with an energy far surpassing all expectations." In the twentieth century, Edmund Morgan maintained that "if one were to make a list of the great men of American history, . . . an astonishingly large proportion would be found whose careers began or culminated in the Revolution." He thought that it would be hard "to find in all the rest of American history more than two or three men to rank with Washington, Franklin, Jefferson, Hamilton, Madison, or John Adams."

The first presidents had struggled though. Seymour Martin Lipset in *The First New Nation* has observed that "a backward glance into our own past should destroy the notion that the United States proceeded easily toward the establishment of democratic political institutions." He elaborated, "It took time to institutionalize values, beliefs, and practices, and there were many incidents that revealed how fragile the commitments to democracy and nationalism really were." Lipset concluded, "But it was from the crucible of confusion and conflict that values and goals became defined, issues carved out, positions taken, in short *an identity established*. For countries, like people, are not handed identities at birth but acquire them through the arduous process of 'growing up,' a process which is a notoriously painful affair."

Leaders at the end of the first generation of the US presidency, however, found widespread agreement that the struggle had been worthwhile. In his final message to Congress in December 1824, James Monroe had reported that the United States was "in the highest degree prosperous and happy," adding that "there is no object which as a people we do not possess, or which is not within our reach." He concluded, "From the present prosperous and happy state I derive a gratification which I cannot express. That these blessings may be preserved and perpetuated will be the object of my fervent and unceasing prayers to the Supreme Ruler of the Universe." The nation found this assessment credible and the sentiments congenial.

Acknowledgments

No writer could ask for more constant support than my editor at Oxford University Press, Nancy Toff, has provided me. More recently, Chelsea Hogue at OUP has skillfully facilitated getting my manuscript to readers. Koperundevi Pugazhenthi has expedited production at a dazzlingly rapid pace, and Leslie Anglin gave the manuscript a professional final read-through while deftly supervising the placement of illustrations. By photocopying reams of research materials for me, month in, month out, my dear friend Jo Sanders has been indispensable.

As I indicated in the dedication, my greatest debt is to Jean Anne Leuchtenburg, whose contribution was far greater than her yeoman work in transferring my penciled paragraphs to a computer. She could always be counted on for a timely prod, especially during the distracting years of the pandemic when much of the manuscript was drafted. Her most important role was as stylist. An instructor in English at the University of Texas and the University of Akron and Publications Director at the National Humanities Center in past years, she repeatedly asked me gently as I was writing this book, "Do you think it might be better to say instead . . . ?"

Selected Bibliography

Abernethy, Thomas P. *The Burr Conspiracy*. New York: Oxford University Press, 1954.

Adams, Henry. *History of the United States of America during the Administrations of Thomas Jefferson*. New York: Library of America, 1986.

Adams, Henry. *History of the United States of America during the Administrations of James Madison*. New York: Library of America, 1986.

Allgor, Catherine. *Parlor Politics: In Which the Ladies of Washington Help Build a City and a Government*. Charlottesville: University of Virginia Press, 2000.

Ammon, Harry. *James Monroe: The Quest for National Identity*. Charlottesville: University of Virginia Press, 1990.

Appleby, Joyce. *Inheriting the Revolution: The First Generation of Americans*. Cambridge, MA: Belknap Press of Harvard University Press, 2000.

Appleby, Joyce. *Thomas Jefferson*. New York: Times Books/Henry Holt, 2003.

Arendt, Hannah. *On Revolution*. New York: Penguin, 2006.

Avlon, John. *Washington's Farewell: The Founding Father's Warning to Future Generations*. New York: Simon & Schuster, 2017.

Bailey, Jeremy D. *Thomas Jefferson and Executive Power*. New York: Cambridge University Press, 2007.

Bailey, Thomas A. *Presidential Greatness: The Image and the Man from George Washington to the Present*. New York: Appleton-Century-Crofts, 1966.

Bailyn, Bernard. *To Begin the World Anew: The Genius and Ambiguities of the American Founders*. New York: Knopf, 2003.

Bailyn, Bernard. *The Origins of American Politics*. New York: Vintage Books, 1968.

Banner, James M., Jr., *To the Hartford Convention: The Federalists and the Origins of Party Politics in Massachusetts, 1789–1815*. New York: Knopf, 1970.

Banning, Lance. *The Jeffersonian Persuasion: Evolution of a Party Ideology*. Ithaca, NY: Cornell University Press, 1978.

Banning, Lance. *The Sacred Fire of Liberty: James Madison and the Founding of the Federal Republic*. Ithaca, NY: Cornell University Press, 1995.

Barbash, Fred. *The Founding: A Dramatic Account of the Writing of the Constitution.* New York: Linden Press/Simon & Schuster, 1987.

Barber, James David. *The Presidential Character.* Englewood Cliffs, NJ: Prentice-Hall, 1972.

Barron, David J. *Waging War: The Clash between Presidents and Congress, 1776 to ISIS.* New York: Simon & Schuster, 2016.

Beeman, Richard. *Plain, Honest Men: The Making of the Constitution.* New York: Random House, 2010.

Beeman, Richard, Stephen Botein, and Edward C. Carter II, eds. *Beyond Confederation: Origins of the Constitution and American National Identity.* Chapel Hill: University of North Carolina Press, 1987.

Bemis, Samuel Flagg. *John Quincy Adams and the Foundations of American Foreign Policy.* New York: Knopf, 1951.

Berkin, Carol. *A Brilliant Solution: Inventing the American Constitution.* New York: Harcourt Brace, 2002.

Bernstein, R. B. *The Education of John Adams.* New York: Oxford University Press, 2020.

Bernstein, R. B. *The Founding Fathers Reconsidered.* New York: Oxford University Press, 2009.

Bernstein, R. B. *Thomas Jefferson.* New York: Oxford University Press, 2003.

Bernstein, Richard B., with Kym S. Rice. *Are We to Be a Nation?: The Making of the Constitution.* Cambridge, MA: Harvard University Press, 1987.

Beschloss, Michael. *Presidents of War: The Epic Story, from 1807 to Modern Times.* New York: Broadway Books, 2018.

Binkley, Wilfred, E. *The President and Congress.* New York: Vintage, 1962.

Boles, John B. *Jefferson: Architect of American Liberty.* New York: Basic Books, 2017.

Borden, Morton, ed. *America's Eleven Greatest Presidents.* Chicago: Rand McNally, 1971.

Borneman, Walter R. *1812: The War That Forged a Nation.* New York: HarperCollins, 2004.

Bowen, Catherine Drinker. *Miracle at Philadelphia: The Story of the Constitutional Convention, May to September 1787.* Boston: Little, Brown, 1986.

Brant, Irving. *James Madison.* 6 vols. Indianapolis, IN: Bobbs-Merrill, 1941.

Breen, T. H. *George Washington's Journey: The President Forges a New Nation.* New York: Simon & Schuster, 2016.

Broadwater, Jeff. *James Madison: A Son of Virginia and a Founder of the Nation.* Chapel Hill: University of North Carolina Press, 2012.

Brookhiser, Richard. *Founding Father: Rediscovering George Washington.* New York: Simon & Schuster, 1996.

Brookhiser, Richard. *Gentleman Revolutionary: Gouverneur Morris, the Rake Who Wrote the Constitution*. New York: Free Press, 2003.

Brown, Ralph Adams. *The Presidency of John Adams*. Lawrence: University Press of Kansas, 1975.

Brown, Roger H. *The Republic in Peril: 1812*. New York: Norton, 1971.

Brown, Stuart Gerry. *The American Presidency: Leadership, Partisanship, and Popularity*. New York: Macmillan, 1966.

Bryan, William Alfred. *George Washington in American Literature, 1775–1865*. Westport, CT: Greenwood Press, 1952.

Buel, Richard, Jr. *America on the Brink: How the Political Struggle over the War of 1812 Almost Destroyed the Young Republic*. New York: Palgrave Macmillan, 2005.

Buel, Richard, Jr. *Securing the Revolution: Ideology in American Politics, 1789–1815*. Ithaca, NY: Cornell University Press, 1972.

Burns, James MacGregor, and Susan Dunn. *George Washington*. New York: Times Books/Henry Holt, 2004.

Burstein, Andrew. *America's Jubilee*. New York: Vintage Books, 2002.

Butterfield, L. H., ed. *The Adams Papers: Adams Family Correspondence*. 11 vols. Cambridge, MA: Belknap Press of Harvard University Press, 1963.

Caraley, Demetrios, ed. *The President's War Powers: From the Federalists to Reagan*. New York: Academy of Political Science, 1984.

Caroli, Betty Boyd. *First Ladies: From Martha Washington to Michelle Obama*. 5th ed. New York: Oxford University Press, 2019.

Chambers, William Nisbet. *Political Parties in a New Nation: The American Experience, 1776–1809*. New York: Oxford University Press, 1963.

Chernow, Ron. *Alexander Hamilton*. New York: Penguin, 2005.

Chernow, Ron. *Washington: A Life*. New York: Penguin, 2010.

Chinard, Gilbert. *Honest John Adams*. Boston: Little, Brown, 1933.

Cogliano, Francis D. *Emperor of Liberty: Thomas Jefferson's Foreign Policy*. New Haven, CT: Yale University Press, 2014.

Collier, Christopher, and James Lincoln Collier. *Decision in Philadelphia: The Constitutional Convention of 1787*. New York: Ballantine Books, Random House, 2007.

Cooper, William J. *The Lost Founding Father: John Quincy Adams and the Transformation of American Politics*. New York: Liveright, 2017.

Corwin, Edward S. *The President: Office and Powers, 1787–1984: A History and Analysis of Practice and Opinion*. New York: New York University Press, 1984.

Cronin, Thomas E., ed. *Inventing the American Presidency*. Lawrence: University Press of Kansas, 1989.

Cunliffe, Marcus. *George Washington: Man and Monument.* New York: New American Library, 1958.

Cunliffe, Marcus. *The Nation Takes Shape, 1789–1837.* Chicago: University of Chicago Press, 1959.

Cunningham, Noble E., Jr. *The Presidency of James Monroe.* Lawrence: University Press of Kansas, 1996.

Cunningham, Noble E., Jr. *The Process of Government under Jefferson.* Princeton, NJ: Princeton University Press, 1978.

Cunningham, Noble E., Jr. *In Pursuit of Reason: The Life of Thomas Jefferson.* Baton Rouge: Louisiana State University Press, 1987.

Dangerfield, George. *The Awakening of American Nationalism, 1815–1828.* New York: Harper & Row, 1965.

Dangerfield, George. *The Era of Good Feelings.* New York: Harcourt, Brace & World, 1952.

DeConde, Alexander. *The Quasi-War: The Politics and Diplomacy of the Undeclared War with France, 1797–1801.* New York: Charles Scribner's Sons, 1966.

Diggins, John Patrick. *John Adams.* New York: Times Books/Henry Holt, 2003.

Elkins, Stanley, and Eric McKitrick. *The Age of Federalism: The Early American Republic, 1788–1800.* New York: Oxford University Press, 1993.

Ellis, Joseph J. *American Creation: Triumphs and Tragedies at the Founding of the Republic.* New York: Random House, 2007.

Ellis, Joseph J. *American Dialogue: The Founders and Us.* New York: Knopf, 2018.

Ellis, Joseph J. *American Sphinx: The Character of Thomas Jefferson.* New York: Vintage Books, 1998.

Ellis, Joseph J. *First Family: Abigail and John Adams.* New York: Vintage Books, 2010.

Ellis, Joseph J. *The Founding Brothers: The Revolutionary Generation.* New York: Vintage Books, 2002.

Ellis, Joseph J. *His Excellency: George Washington.* New York: Penguin, 2005.

Ellis, Joseph J. *Passionate Sage: The Character and Legacy of John Adams.* New York: Norton, 1993.

Ellis, Joseph J. *The Quartet: Orchestrating the Second American Revolution, 1783–1789.* New York: Knopf, 2015.

Ellis, Richard E. *The Jeffersonian Crisis: Courts and Politics in the Young Republic.* New York: Oxford University Press, 1971.

Ellis, Richard E., ed. *Founding the American Presidency.* Lanham, MD: Rowman & Littlefield, 1999.

Ellis, Richard E., and Aaron Wildavsky. *Dilemmas of Presidential Leadership: From Washington through Lincoln.* New Brunswick, NJ: Transaction Publishers, 1989.

Elkins, Stanley, and Eric McKitrick. *The Age of Federalism: The Early American Republic, 1788–1800*. New York: Oxford University Press, 1993.

Farrand, Max, ed. *The Records of the Federal Convention*. 3 vols. New Haven, CT: Yale University Press, 1911.

Feldman, Noah. *The Three Lives of James Madison*. New York: Random House, 2017.

Feller, Daniel. *The Jacksonian Promise: America, 1815–1840*. Baltimore: Johns Hopkins University Press, 1995.

Ferling, John. *Adams vs. Jefferson: The Tumultuous Election of 1800*. New York: Oxford University Press, 2004.

Ferling, John. *The Ascent of George Washington: The Hidden Political Genius of an American Icon*. New York: Bloomsbury, 2009.

Ferling, John. *Jefferson and Hamilton: The Rivalry That Forged a Nation*. New York: Bloomsbury, 2013.

Ferling, John. *A Leap in the Dark: The Struggle to Create the American Republic*. New York: Oxford University Press, 2003.

Flexner, James Thomas. *Washington: The Indispensable Man*. New York: Little, Brown, 1974.

Forbes, Robert Pierce. *The Missouri Compromise and Its Aftermath*. Chapel Hill: University of North Carolina Press, 2007.

Freehling, William W. *Prelude to Civil War: The Nullification Controversy in South Carolina, 1818–1836*. New York: Oxford University Press, 1992.

Freeman, Douglas Southall. *Washington*. Abridged by Richard Harwell. New York: Charles Scribner's Sons, 1968.

Goldsmith, William M. *The Growth of Presidential Power: A Documented History*. New York: Chelsea House, 1974.

Gordon-Reed, Annette, and Peter S. Onuf. *"Most Blessed of the Patriarchs": Thomas Jefferson and the Empire of the Imagination*. New York: Liveright, 2016.

Gould, Lewis L., ed. *American First Ladies: Their Lives and Their Legacy*. New York: Routledge, 1996.

Graff, Henry F., ed. *The Presidents: A Reference History*. New York: Charles Scribner's Sons, 1984.

Green, Constance McLaughlin. *Washington: A History of the Capital, 1800–1950*. Princeton, NJ: Princeton University Press, 1976.

Greenstein, Fred. *Inventing the Job of President: Leadership Style from George Washington to Andrew Jackson*. Princeton, NJ: Princeton University Press, 2009.

Groom, Winston. *The Patriots: Alexander Hamilton, Thomas Jefferson, John Adams, and the Making of America*. Washington, DC: National Geographic, 2020.

Gutzman, Kevin R. C. *The Jeffersonians: The Visionary Presidencies of Jefferson, Madison, and Monroe.* New York: St. Martin's Press, 2022.

Hargreaves, Mary W. M. *The Presidency of John Quincy Adams.* Lawrence: University Press of Kansas, 1985.

Harriger, Katy J. *Separation of Powers: Documents and Commentary.* Washington, DC: CQ Press, 2003.

Hart, James. *American Presidency in Action, 1789: A Study in Constitutional History.* New York: Macmillan, 1948.

Heale, M. J. *The Presidential Quest: Candidates and Images in American Political Culture, 1787–1852.* London: Longman, 1982.

Heidler, David S., and Jeanne T. Heidler. *Washington's Circle: The Creation of the President.* New York: Random House, 2016.

Henkin, Louis. *Foreign Affairs and the Constitution.* New York: Norton, 1972.

Henriques, Peter R. *Realistic Visionary: A Portrait of George Washington.* Charlottesville: University of Virginia Press, 2006.

Herrick, Carole L. *August 24, 1814: Washington in Flames.* Falls Church, VA: Higher Education Publications, 2005.

Herring, George. *From Colony to Superpower: U.S. Foreign Relations since 1776.* New York: Oxford University Press, 2011.

Hickey, Donald. *The War of 1812: A Forgotten Conflict.* Urbana: University of Illinois Press, 2012.

Higginbotham, Don. *George Washington: Uniting a Nation.* Lanham, MD: Rowman & Littlefield, 2002.

Higginbotham, Don, ed. *George Washington Reconsidered.* Charlottesville: University of Virginia Press, 2001.

Horn, Jonathan. *Washington's End: The Final Years and Forgotten Struggle.* New York: Scribner, 2020.

Howe, Daniel Walker. *What Hath God Wrought: The Transformation of America, 1815–1848.* New York: Oxford University Press, 2007.

Hunt, Gaillard. *The Life of James Madison.* New York: Doubleday, Page & Co., 1902.

Isenberg, Nancy. *Fallen Founder: The Life of Aaron Burr.* New York: Penguin, 2007.

Isenberg, Nancy, and Andrew Burstein. *The Problem of Democracy: The Presidents Adams Confront the Cult of Personality.* New York: Penguin, 2019.

Jillson, Calvin C. *Constitution Making: Conflict and Consensus in the Federal Convention of 1787.* New York: Agathon Press, 2002.

Johnstone, Robert M., Jr. *Jefferson and the Presidency: Leadership in the Young Republic.* Ithaca, NY: Cornell University Press, 1978.

Kallenbach, Joseph E. *The American Chief Executive: The Presidency and the Governorship*. New York: Harper & Row, 1966.

Kaminski, John P., ed. *The Founders on the Founders: Word Portraits from the American Revolutionary Era*. Charlottesville: University of Virginia Press, 2008.

Kaplan, Fred. *John Quincy Adams: American Visionary*. New York: HarperCollins, 2014.

Kelley, Alfred H., and Winfred A. Harbison. *The American Constitution: Its Origins and Development*. New York: Norton, 1976.

Ketcham, Ralph. *James Madison: A Biography*. Charlottesville: University of Virginia Press, 1990.

Ketcham, Ralph. *Presidents above Party: The First American Presidency, 1789– 1829*. Chapel Hill: University of North Carolina Press and Institute of Early American History and Culture, 1984.

Ketcham, Ralph, ed. *The Anti-Federalist Papers and the Constitutional Convention Debates*. New York: Signet, 2003.

Kilmeade, Brian, and Don Yaeger. *Thomas Jefferson and the Tripoli Pirates: The Forgotten War that Changed American History*. New York: Sentinel, 2016.

Klotter, James C. *Henry Clay: The Man Who Would Be President*. New York: Oxford University Press, 2018.

Kukla, Jon. *A Wilderness So Immense: The Louisiana Purchase and the Destiny of America*. New York: Random House, 2003.

Kurtz, Stephen G. *The Presidency of John Adams: The Collapse of Federalism, 1795–1800*. Philadelphia: University of Pennsylvania Press, 1957.

Lamb, Brian, Susan Swain, and C-SPAN, eds. *The Presidents: Noted Historians Rank America's Best—and Worst—Chief Executives*. New York: Public Affairs, 2019.

Landy, Marc, and Sidney M. Milkis. *Presidential Greatness*. Lawrence: University Press of Kansas, 2000.

Larson, Edward J. *A Magnificent Catastrophe: The Tumultuous Election of 1800: America's First Presidential Campaign*. New York: Simon & Schuster, 2007.

Larson, Edward J. *The Return of George Washington, 1783–1789*. New York: HarperCollins, 2014.

Larson, Edward J., and Michael P. Winship. *The Constitutional Convention: A Narrative History from the Notes of James Madison*. New York: Modern Library, 2005.

Levin, Phyllis Lee. *Abigail Adams: A Biography*. New York: St. Martin's Press, 1987.

Levy, Leonard W. *Jefferson and Civil Liberties: The Darker Side*. Cambridge, MA: Harvard University Press, 1963.

Lipset, Seymour Martin. *The First New Nation: The United States in Historical and Comparative Perspective*. New York: Norton, 1973.

Longmore, Paul K. *The Invention of George Washington*. Charlottesville: University of Virginia Press, 1999.

Magill, Frank N., ed. *The American Presidents: The Office and the Men*, vol. 1. Pasadena, CA: Salem Press, 1986.

Malone, Dumas. *Jefferson and His Time*. 6 vols. Boston: Little, Brown, 1948–1981.

May, Ernest R., ed. *The Ultimate Decision: The President as Commander in Chief*. New York: Braziller, 1960.

McCoy, Drew R. *The Last of the Fathers: James Madison and the Republican Legacy*. New York: Cambridge University Press, 1989.

McCullough, David. *John Adams*. New York: Simon & Schuster, 2001.

Meacham, Jon. *Thomas Jefferson: The Art of Power*. New York: Random House, 2012.

Milkis, Sidney M., and Michael Nelson. *The American Presidency: Origins and Development, 1776–2014*. Los Angeles: Sage, 2016.

Miller, John C. *Alexander Hamilton: Portrait in Paradox*. Old Saybrook, CT: Konecky & Konecky, 1959.

Miller, John C. *The Federalist Era: 1789–1801*. New York: Harper & Row, 1963.

Milton, George Fort. *The Use of Presidential Power, 1789–1943*. Boston: Little, Brown, 1944.

Miroff, Bruce. *Icons of Democracy: American Leaders as Heroes, Aristocrats, Dissenters, and Democrats*. Lawrence: University Press of Kansas, 2000.

Morgan, Edmund S. *The Genius of George Washington*. New York: Norton, 1980.

Morgan, Edmund S. *The Meaning of Independence: John Adams, George Washington, and Thomas Jefferson*. Charlottesville: University of Virginia Press, 1976.

Morris, Richard B. *The Forging of the Union, 1781–1789*. New York: Harper & Row, 1987.

Nagel, Paul C. *John Quincy Adams: A Public Life, A Private Life*. Cambridge, MA: Harvard University Press, 1997.

Onuf, Peter S. *Jefferson's Empire: The Language of American Nationhood*. Charlottesville: University Press of Virginia, 2000.

Onuf, Peter S., ed. *Jeffersonian Legacies*. Charlottesville: University of Virginia Press, 1993.

Parsons, Lynn Hudson. *The Birth of Modern Politics: Andrew Jackson, John Quincy Adams, and the Election of 1828*. New York: Oxford University Press, 2009.

Parsons, Lynn Hudson. *John Quincy Adams*. Lanham, MD: Rowman & Littlefield, 2001.

Perkins, Bradford. *The Creation of a Republican Empire, 1776–1865.* Cambridge, England: Cambridge University Press, 1993.

Perkins, Bradford. *Prologue to War: England and the United States, 1805–1812.* Berkeley: University of California Press, 1961.

Peterson, Merrill. *The Jefferson Image in the American Mind.* New York: Oxford University Press, 1960.

Peterson, Merrill. *Thomas Jefferson and the New Nation.* New York: Oxford University Press, 1970.

Phelps, Glenn A. *George Washington and American Constitutionalism.* Lawrence: University Press of Kansas, 1993.

Pious, Richard M. *The American Presidency.* New York: Basic Books, 1979.

Pious, Richard M. *The Presidency.* Boston: Allyn & Bacon, 1995.

Pitch, Anthony S. *The Burning of Washington: The British Invasion of 1814.* Annapolis, MD: Naval Institute Press, 1998.

Pollard, James E. *The Presidents and the Press.* New York: Macmillan, 1947.

Pyle, Christopher H., and Richard M. Pious. *The President, Congress, and the Constitution.* New York: Free Press/Macmillan, 1984.

Rakove, Jack N. *James Madison and the Creation of the American Republic.* New York: Pearson/Longman, 2007.

Rakove, Jack N. *Original Meanings: Politics and Ideas in the Making of the Constitution.* New York: Vintage Books, 1997.

Randall, Willard Sterne. *Unshackling America: How the War of 1812 Truly Ended the American Revolution.* New York: St. Martin's Press, 2017.

Raphael, Ray. *Mr. President: How and Why the Founders Created a Chief Executive.* New York: Vintage Books, 2013.

Remini, Robert V. *Andrew Jackson and the Course of American Freedom, 1822–1832.* New York: Harper & Row, 1981.

Remini, Robert V. *John Quincy Adams.* New York: Times Books/Henry Holt, 2002.

Riccards, Michael P. *A Republic, If You Can Keep It: The Foundation of the American Presidency, 1700–1800.* Westport, CT: Greenwood Press, 1987.

Richards, Leonard L. *Shays's Rebellion: The American Revolution's Final Battle.* Philadelphia: University of Pennsylvania Press, 2002.

Robinson, Donald L. *"To the Best of My Ability": The Presidency and the Constitution.* New York: Norton, 1987.

Rossiter, Clinton L. *1787: The Grand Convention.* New York: Macmillan, 1966.

Rutland, Robert Allen. *James Madison: The Founding Father.* New York: Macmillan, 1987.

Rutland, Robert Allen. *The Presidency of James Madison.* Lawrence: University Press of Kansas, 1990.

Schlesinger, Arthur M., Jr., and Fred L. Israel, eds. *History of American Presidential Elections, 1789–1969*. New York: Chelsea House, 1985.

Schwartz, Barry. *George Washington: The Making of an American Symbol*. Ithaca, NY: Cornell University Press, 1987.

Seale, William. *The President's House: A History*, vol. 1. Washington, DC: White House Historical Association with the cooperation of the National Geographic Society, 1986.

Sedgwick, John. *War of Two: Alexander Hamilton, Aaron Burr, and the Duel That Stunned the Nation*. New York: Penguin Random House, 2015.

Shade, William G., Ballard C. Campbell, and Craig R. Coenen, eds. *American Presidential Campaigns and Elections*. Armonk, NY: Sharpe Reference, 2003.

Sharp, James Roger. *American Politics in the Early Republic: The New Nation in Crisis*. New Haven, CT: Yale University Press, 1993.

Signer, Michael. *Becoming Madison: The Extraordinary Origins of the Least Likely Founding Father*. New York: PublicAffairs, 2015.

Skowronek, Stephen. *The Politics Presidents Make: Leadership from John Adams to George Bush*. Cambridge, MA: Belknap Press of Harvard University Press, 1993.

Slaughter, Thomas. *The Whiskey Rebellion: Frontier Epilogue to the American Revolution*. New York: Oxford University Press, 1986.

Smith, Page. *John Adams*. 2 vols. Garden City, NY: Doubleday, 1962.

Smith, Richard Norton. *Patriarch: George Washington and the New American Nation*. Boston: Houghton Mifflin, 1993.

Snow, Peter. *When Britain Burned the White House: The 1814 Invasion of Washington*. New York: Thomas Dunne Books/St. Martin's Press, 2014.

Stagg, J. C. A. *Mr. Madison's War: Politics, Diplomacy and Warfare in the Early American Republic, 1783–1830*. Princeton, NJ: Princeton University Press, 1983.

Steele, Brian. *Thomas Jefferson and American Nationhood*. New York: Cambridge University Press, 2012.

Stewart, David O. *The Summer of 1787: The Men Who Invented the Constitution*. New York: Simon & Schuster, 2007.

Styron, Arthur. *The Last of the Cocked Hats: James Monroe and the Virginia Dynasty*. Norman: University of Oklahoma Press, 1945.

Swain, Susan, and C-SPAN. *First Ladies: Presidential Historians on the Lives of 45 Iconic American Women*. New York: Public Affairs, 2015.

Syrett, Harold C., and Jacob E. Cooke, eds. *The Papers of Alexander Hamilton*. 17 vols. New York: Columbia University Press, 1961.

Tatalovich, Raymond, and Thomas S. Engeman. *The Presidency and Political Science: Two Hundred Years of Constitutional Debate*. Baltimore: Johns Hopkins University Press, 2003.

Taylor, Alan. *American Revolutions: A Continental History, 1750–1804*. New York: Norton, 2016.

Tebbel, John, and Sarah Miles Watts. *The Press and the Presidency: From George Washington to Ronald Reagan*. New York: Oxford University Press, 1985.

Thach, Charles C., Jr. *The Creation of the Presidency: 1775–1789: A Study in Constitutional History*. Baltimore: Johns Hopkins University Press, 1923.

Tourtellot, Arthur Bernon, ed. *The Presidents on the Presidency*. Garden City, NY: Doubleday, 1960.

Traub, James. *John Quincy Adams: Militant Spirit*. New York: Basic Books, 2016.

Tulis, Jeffrey K. *The Rhetorical Presidency*. Princeton, NJ: Princeton University Press, 2016.

Unger, Harlow Giles. *The Last Founding Father: James Monroe and a Nation's Call to Greatness*. Philadelphia: Da Capo Press, 2009.

Unger, Harlow Giles. *"Mr. President": George Washington and the Making of the Nation's Highest Office*. Philadelphia: Da Capo Press, 2013.

Urofsky, Melvin I., and Paul Finkelman. *A March of Liberty: A Constitutional History of the United States*, vol. 1. New York: Oxford University Press, 2002.

Waldstreicher, David. *In the Midst of Perpetual Fetes: The Making of American Nationalism*. Chapel Hill: University of North Carolina Press, 1997.

Waldstreicher, David, and Matthew Mason. *John Quincy Adams and the Politics of Slavery*. New York: Oxford University Press, 2016.

Ward, John William. *Andrew Jackson: Symbol for an Age*. New York: Oxford University Press, 1985.

Watson, Harry L. *Liberty and Power: The Politics of Jacksonian America*. New York: Hill and Wang, 2006.

White, Leonard D. *The Federalists: A Study in Administrative History*. Westport, CT: Greenwood Press, 1978.

White, Leonard D. *The Jeffersonians: A Study in Administrative History, 1801–1829*. New York: Macmillan, 1951.

Wiebe, Robert H. *The Opening of American Society: From the Adoption of the Constitution to the Eve of Disunion*. New York: Knopf, 1984.

Wilentz, Sean. *The Rise of American Democracy: Jefferson to Lincoln*. New York: Norton, 2005.

Wills, Garry. *Cincinnatus: George Washington and the Enlightenment*. Garden City, NY: Doubleday, 1984.

Wills, Garry. *James Madison*. New York: Times Books/Henry Holt, 2002.

Wood, Gordon S. *The Creation of the American Republic, 1776–1787*. Chapel Hill: University of North Carolina Press, 1998.

Wood, Gordon S. *Empire of Liberty: A History of the Early Republic, 1789–1815*. New York: Oxford University Press, 2009.

Wood, Gordon S. *Friends Divided: John Adams and Thomas Jefferson*. New York: Penguin, 2017.

Wood, Gordon S. *Power and Liberty: Constitutionalism in the American Revolution*. New York: Oxford University Press, 2021.

Wood, Gordon S. *Revolutionary Characters: What Made the Founders Different*. New York: Penguin, 2006.

Yarbrough, Jean. *American Virtues: Thomas Jefferson on the Character of a Free People*. Lawrence: University Press of Kansas, 1998.

Young, James Sterling. *The Washington Community, 1800–1828*. New York: Columbia University Press, 1966.

Index

For the benefit of digital users, indexed terms that span two pages (e.g., 52–53) may, on occasion, appear on only one of those pages.

Figures are indicated by an italic *f* following the page number.